# Sonny Boy and Jewel Griffin

Tales of rodeoing, hard drinking and
bar room brawls, horse races, hunt
clubs, moonshine and running from
revenuers, raising cattle, butchering
meat, keeping families close, working
hard, and holding on tight to faith.

## MIKE TOLBERT

outskirts
press

# TABLE OF CONTENTS

Weaving a Quilt Cut from the Cloth of Two Legends ......... 1

Griffin Roots Deep in the Land ......... 5

Diamond in the Rough a Real Jewel ......... 14

The Gentle Cowboy Giant ......... 26

Two Rough and Tumble Gals Become Fabled Horse Women ......... 41

Young Rural Pioneers to Big Time Ranchers ......... 49

Make Pulpwood or Make Whiskey. ......... 58

This Acorn Didn't Fall Far From the Tree ......... 67

Butchering Meat: Family Tradition and a Science ......... 75

Riding, Working, No Nonsense ......... 79

Dreaming of Horses Turns into Nightmare ......... 87

Growing Up Grandchildren of Diamond D Ranch ......... 99

Do it First, Do it Well…or Else ......... 108

San Marco to Diamond D to the Courthouse ......... 114

Sonny Boy and Jim Kittrell: the "Hatfields and McCoys" ......... 122

Sonny Boy, the Hunting Guru ......... 131

Common Sense Better than Book Learning ......... 139

Scaring the Booze Out of Sonny Boy ......... 147

Hog Dogs, Hard Work, and Hell Raising Cowboys ......... 151

Battling Jacksonville's Powerful to Save the Westside ......... 159

Ranch Grows, Values Remain ......... 169

"This is not just land. This is the Griffins." ......... 178

Yummy. Yummy. Jewel's Favorite Recipes ......... 185

# Weaving a Quilt Cut from the Cloth of Two Legends

*"All of my life I've heard about the 'Salt of the Earth.' For the last few weeks, talking to these wonderful people, I have tasted that salt."*

**Over three years** ago, Michael Griffin and I had lunch at Everybody's Cafe in Baldwin, Florida. He wanted to talk to me about writing a book about his parents, Jewel and Sonny Boy Griffin. Michael wanted to capture for future generations of Griffins the values, struggles, perseverance, and strengths that is the Griffin legacy, as well as the history of Diamond D Ranch.

For some reason, the idea was put on the back burner. That was prior to his dad's passing in in January 2018.

In the summer of 2021, Michael renewed the conversation and we agreed to get started.

I already knew of Sonny Boy and Jewel through Jacksonville politics.

In addition, my wife Annette and I boarded horses at Diamond D in the early 2000s, before we moved to our own horse farm in Brooksville, Florida.

I'll never forget the day Annette phoned the ranch to ask about boarding. She told me she had received a recorded message: "Thanks for calling Diamond D Ranch, home of Sonny Boy and Ms. Jewel." Annette thought Sonny Boy and Jewel were horses.

When we first arrived as boarders at Diamond D, Annette was a new rider, anxious to learn and she was somewhat fearless. Like so many women at Diamond D before her, she took directly to Jewel, sought her advice and counsel, and listened to her every word.

During one hot week in July that first summer, along with Greg and Katherine McCandless, Annette attended a summer horse camp for adults conducted by the Griffin's daughter, Cathy. Like her mother, Cathy Melton is a master horse person. Like her dad, she's a person of few words, and many of them come out pretty hard.

When Annette would come home after a long day at camp in the boiling summer sun, having been barked at for hours by Cathy, the drill sergeant, I would ask why she was going back the next day?

Then there was the day that she told me Cathy had taught her how to clean a horse's sheath, a pocket of skin that protects the penis of the horse. It's an unpleasant task not usually embraced by either the rider or the horse.

Because of my involvement in the community since the early 1970s, I thought I knew something about Jacksonville's westside, and how different it is from much of the rest of Jacksonville. But I had no idea about the unique, wild westside world of the forties, fifties, sixties, and seventies that I was about to hear.

The westside has long been a blue-collar community where hard-working families have been stewards of the earth, lived off the land, and on occasion brewed moonshine whiskey to help them make a living. For generations, people raised in west Jacksonville have generally remained in west Jacksonville, often not far from where they were raised, and still surrounded by the families, friends, and institutions they knew growing up.

As I was just getting started, a friend asked what I thought this book would eventually be about. I said it probably would be stories about rodeoing, racing horses, making moonshine, running from revenuers, penning cows, racing stock cars, hard drinking, bar room brawls, keeping families together, working hard, and holding on tight to faith.

Before I could begin writing, I needed to interview people who know the Griffins well. The list included Griffin family members, children, grandchildren, sisters, cousins. It was a rich list provided by Ms. Jewel and Michael that included some of Ms. Jewel's horse friends, and a few of Sonny Boy's remaining hunting and drinking buddies, some who had witnessed the wrath of his temper and knew stories of some of his fabled bar fights.

About a month after I started the interviews, I told a friend, "All of my life I've heard about the 'Salt of the Earth.' For the last few weeks, talking to these wonderful people, I have tasted that salt."

In every conversation, I could the feel joy as they told their stories about the Griffins and Diamond D. The memories were vivid, as if what they were describing had just happened, not years ago. That openness and eagerness to share with me was invaluable.

I explained to each person that I'm a storyteller, not an historian. My mission was simple: take their own personal memories and weave them into a quilt that tells in a warm, inspiring, and sometimes humorous way the story of this legendary couple.

I hope I've done that.

Finally, I want to thank Michael and his wife, Galynna, who were the inspiration behind Sonny Boy and Jewel, and whose family asked the book to be dedicated to them.

Mike Tolbert

# Griffin Roots Deep in the Land

*"Daddy and Momma Griffin were both from large families. Momma Griffin came from a family of 18 boys and girls, Daddy Griffin came from nine boys and girls. Daddy Griffin didn't want a large family because he came from one and knew the hardships a big family can have."*

**Seventy-year-old Terry Freeman** is a nephew of Jewel and Sonny Boy Griffin. He's the son of Sonny Boy's sister, Virginia Griffin Thornton. Freeman's grandparents were Dewey and Eva Griffin, the parents of Sonny Boy.

Freeman's also the keeper and curator of the Griffin family history.

"My grandfather (Daddy Griffin) was from Thomasville, Ga., and my grandmother (Momma Griffin) was from Cairo," said Freeman. The two small Georgia towns are less than 15 miles apart. "They were both from families that farmed."

Both of Sonny Boy's parents grew up in "very large families, and they were the first to move to Florida." Others followed, often staying with the Griffins while they looked for work and places to live. "It was brothers and sisters, children, grandchildren," said Freeman. "My grandmother used to say she never had her husband to herself because there was always somebody there."

Dewey Griffin was a lot like his own dad, James F. Griffin, Freeman's great grandfather. James F. Griffin trained hunting dogs for the plantations around the Thomasville area. "I always remember them saying he was a man of few words, and when he talked, you needed to listen."

Freeman's grandfather, Dewey Griffin, "was the same way. He didn't just talk to talk, so when he said something, you needed to listen because you were going to learn something."

Sonny Boy was born Dewey Franklin Griffin and named after his father. But his mother didn't take long to put the handle on the young boy that would be his name and brand for all of his life, "Sonny Boy" Griffin.

"He had bright red hair, and he had such a sunny disposition of as a child that she called him, 'Sonny Boy,' and it stuck," said Freeman.

Freeman said as an adult, Sonny Boy remained, "a very sunny dispositioned individual most of the time. Very seldom did you see the hard side of Uncle Sonny Boy. I've seen him mad, and I've seen him with good reason to be mad. But that's how the Griffins were."

Freeman's mother and Sonny Boy had an older sister, Dorothy. "Daddy and Momma Griffin were both from large families. Momma Griffin came from a family of 18 boys and girls, and Daddy Griffin came from nine boys and girls. "Daddy Griffin didn't want a large family because he knew the hardships a big family can have."

SONNY BOY AND JEWEL GRIFFIN

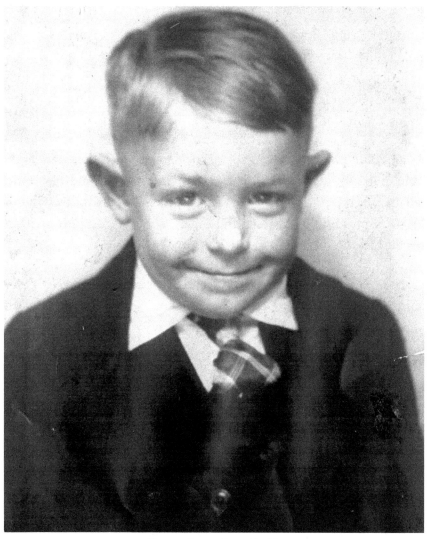

*Young Sonny Boy Griffin*

When Sonny Boy was born on March 7, 1934, his older sisters were teenagers. "He was one of those late-comers," said Freeman. Sonny Boy's arrival made his father, "feel like his dreams had been fulfilled because he got a son."

Up until Sonny Boy's arrival, Freeman's mother, Virginia, was very close to her father. But that changed when Dewey Griffin had the son he badly wanted and cherished, said Freeman. "My mother was jealous of Sonny Boy. He took her place with Daddy Griffin, and I think she always resented it."

As an adult, when Sonny Boy and his dad would have differences, "My mother would get in the thick of it." Freeman said he would tell his mother, "It's none of your business. I can understand if Uncle Sonny Boy starts resenting other people wanting to get into his business."

Freeman said the Griffins, "always played their cards close. They never put their business in the street. They'll tell you what they want you to know. That came from the Griffins way back."

That didn't matter much to his mother, Virginia. "My mother would fight with a circle saw. If she thought it, you knew it." That, Freeman said, "was the Daughtry side coming out." Sonny Boy's mother had been a Daughtry before marrying Dewey Griffin.

"I think Sonny Boy got his feistiness from the Daughtrys."

"My grandmother would fight at the drop of a hat. That's the way it was back then. You fight with one another, but you don't get a divorce." Dewey and Eva Griffin were married 55 years," said Freeman.

When Sonny Boy was young, he lived with his parents on Lenox Avenue in west Jacksonville, closer to downtown than Diamond D.

SONNY BOY AND JEWEL GRIFFIN

The James M. Daughtry family

Sonny Boy with parents, sisters

*Eva, Dewey, Sonny Boy at Lenox Avenue home*

SONNY BOY AND JEWEL GRIFFIN

Mr. Griffin was a butcher and owned a meat market near their house named, "Griffin's Store."

Keep in mind that this period of time was just after the Great Depression and during World War II. Many of the people who shopped at Griffin's Store were poor.

"My grandfather never let anybody go hungry. He said they could pay the next time they came in," said Freeman.

Sonny Boy's mother, Eva, however, felt different. "My grandmother fussed about it," said Freeman. "She said they were in the business to make money and not give things away. But my grandfather would tell her as long as they have money to eat and pay their bills, he would worry about the rest of it."

In addition to selling meat, Mr. Griffin also made and distributed moonshine at Griffin's Store.

Dewey Griffin's moonshining began on a small farm in Sanderson, FL. "He got hooked up with people buying and distributing moonshine around Duval County."

According to Freeman, Mr. Griffin brewed moonshine the same way he butchered meat. "He was known for making extremely good moonshine. He didn't cut corners. He wanted to make sure if his name was on it, it was a good product."

At the store, Mr. Griffin made sure his customers, "didn't have to worry about buying something bad. He wanted to make sure people were satisfied with what he sold them because if they weren't, it was a mark against his name."

It was at Griffin's Store that Sonny Boy learned from his dad how to butcher meat and brew moonshine whiskey, two skills which helped Sonny Boy earn a living and became part of the legacy of his life.

In the 1950's, Mr. Griffin was caught making and selling moonshine by federal revenuers. He spent six months in a federal prison in Tallahassee, FL. When Mr. Griffin was released, Freeman said, "He was in his fifties, and he'd lost a leg in an auto accident. He promised he wouldn't make or sell moonshine anymore."

After his father's death and Diamond D was running well, Freeman said Sonny Boy thought about selling the Ranch and moving to the Thomasville/Cairo area in Georgia where his parents were raised. "But when he got to thinking about it, it was not something he could do."

The first 40 acres at Diamond D were purchased by Mr. Griffin using moonshine profits.

The "D" in Diamond D stands for "Dewey," his father's name.

And, in the final years of their lives, Sonny Boy's mother and father lived at the ranch with Jewel and him.

"This was his daddy's. This was what Dewey Griffin was all about. Diamond D was Sonny Boy's link to Daddy Griffin, and he wanted Daddy Griffin to be proud of him."

# Diamond in the Rough
## a Real Jewel

———～～～———

*"My mother influenced my life greatly. She taught
me the way you should live, and to be thankful for
what you have. My mother had more patience than
anybody I've known in my life. I learned from her to
be kind and treat people like you want to be treated,
always help other people when you could."*

BEFORE TWELVE-YEAR-OLD JEWEL Stoddard and her eleven brothers and
sisters arrived in Jacksonville in 1943, she had already lived with her
parents in nine different towns from Texas to Ohio.

Born in Houston, Texas on June 9, 1936, she lived in Springfield,
Ohio (age two), Galina, Missouri (age three), Galveston, Texas (age
four), Arkana, Arkansas (age six), Pharr, Texas (age eight), Cotter,
Arkansas (age nine), Winter Haven, Florida (age ten), and Sanford,
Florida (age eleven). After arriving in Jacksonville, Jewel never moved
to another city.

*Juanita and Jack Stoddard*

"I had nine brothers and three sisters," she said. "I am number six." Jack and Juanita Stoddard gave each of their thirteen a first name that begins with the letter J, although three of the boys were called by their second name.

In birth order, the thirteen children were: twins Jack Jr. (Jackie) and Janet, born 1930; John (Bill), born 1932; James, born 1933; Jerry, born 1934; Jewel, born 1936; Jeanne (Neni), born 1937; Joe, born 1940; Jay, born 1941; Joy, born 1943; Jan, born 1945; Johnathon (David), born 1946, and Julian (Mark), born 1950.

Jewel's family moved often to follow their father's work, primarily as a truck driver. At times he drove a produce truck, worked in the Galveston and Jacksonville shipyards, and drove piggyback trucks for Kenosha Auto Parts.

*The Stoddard family*

"He was one of those fellas who was a Jack of all trades, but a master of none," Jewel said.

Being constantly uprooted from school didn't bother Jewel too much. "I had so many brothers and sisters it didn't matter that it was hard to make friends. We were very close growing up. We'd take up for each other."

Jeanne Stoddard Jenkins is Jewel's sister. She's one year younger. Because some of the Stoddard children had difficulty pronouncing "Jeanne," she picked up the nickname "Neni," which is how she is still known decades later.

As the two girls grew up moving from place to place, they were very close. "Our house was always in a total state of confusion. When it came to things like bathroom activities, somebody was brushing their teeth, somebody was going to the bathroom, somebody was showering, somebody was combing their hair. It was a wild community there in the morning," said Neni.

*Jewel and Neni with their husbands*

"Some of the children in the family thrived on moving a lot. I don't think it bothered Sissy (Jewel) that much. We had our family, and you sure didn't lack for companionship."

Her mother, Juanita, was a devout Catholic, as is Jewel, christened when the family lived in Springfield, Ohio.

The Stoddard's last child was born in Jacksonville, Florida. Jewel was eleven.

"My mother influenced my life greatly," she said. "She taught me the way you should live, and to be thankful for what you have. My mother had more patience than anybody I've known in my life. I learned from her to be kind and treat people like you want to be treated, always help other people when you could."

Despite having thirteen children of her own to care for, Jewel said, "If there was a wayward kid that didn't have no place to go, she made him a place on the floor and fed him."

Because the Stoddards lived with financial hardships, and Jack Stoddard was often absent, it fell to Juanita to deal with whatever happened with the family. "She was always there for us to get us through anything we needed to get through." She could "fix anything."

When one of Jewel's brothers fell down the stairs and broke his leg, Juanita didn't take him to the doctor. Instead, she set his leg. "You didn't have no welfare or nothing back then," Jewel said. "My momma was proud. She would never have asked. I'm a lot like my mother. I'm proud that I'm like my momma."

Growing up, Neni said her sister Jewel was the "protector. If somebody was mistreating us, or if we skinned our knees, she was always helping us get up and get started."

When they were children, Neni recalled the day she and Jewel were lost on a golf course. "We'd walked one of our little friend's home. We didn't gauge our time and it was getting dark on us. I knew we'd never find our way home, so I sat down on the sandy road and just cried."

Jewel was having none of it. "She snatched me up by the arm and said, 'Neni, get up from there. We're about to run out of daylight, and we don't have time for you to sit down there and cry. Now, get up.' I got up and she held my hand and found our way home."

Over the years, Neni said Jewel has not changed. "She still does that with people all the time. You never know she's there with a helping hand because she does it discreetly. She doesn't like fanfare or acknowledgement."

Sister Joy Stoddard Harmon is seven years younger than Jewel. "She was her own self," said Joy. "I was her responsibility to get ready for school in the morning. She had to get me dressed and get my hair done. She was rough and raked the comb through my hair."

When Joy complained to her mother, Jewel replied, "Well, she's got rats in her hair."

After the Stoddard's arrived in Jacksonville, the family continued to move from place to place, landing first on Marshal Street on the city's northside. Because Jack Stoddard was working at the Jacksonville Shipyards, after a short while the family moved to Hendricks Avenue in south Jacksonville, closer to his work. From Hendricks Avenue, the Stoddards moved to Beaver Street, then to Julington Creek, and finally Memorial Park Road on the westside.

"We just did what we had to do, and I never had any bad feelings about moving. I probably thought everybody lived like that." Afterall, said

Jewel, "A lot of people were poor back then. It wasn't that we were the only people who were poor."

In the seventh grade, when the family lived on Hendricks Avenue, Jewel attended Alfred I. Dupont Jr. High. That's when Juanita Stoddard had her thirteenth and final child, a boy named Julian (Mark).

Her mother had a difficult delivery. "She was very weak. I had to stay home and take care of her and the baby," she remembered. "I can take care of babies. I've been taking care of babies all my life."

Because she wasn't attending school, Jewel said a truant officer came to her house. "Why are you not in school?"

"Well, I took her in there and showed her the reasons I wasn't in school." Afterwards, Jewel said, during the month she was absent, her schoolwork was delivered to the house daily.

As a tenth grader at Lee High School, by now a rising star as a competitive equestrian, Jewel met Sonny Boy Griffin while barrel racing at a rodeo in nearby Callahan in 1953. They dated for six months, going to movies, horse shows, and "riding together a lot."

In the eleventh grade and seventeen-years-old, Jewel quit school to marry nineteen-year-old Sonny Boy.

"We kind of fell in love right away and decided we was the right person for each other. People was telling me, 'Don't marry him. He makes whiskey.' They were telling my momma and daddy not to let me marry him."

None of it deterred Jewel. "They made liquor, but they didn't steal. My husband didn't go to church, but he was a firm believer in God."

1953 - 17 yrs

*17-year-old Jewel Stoddard*

After moving from state to state and neighborhood to neighborhood in Jacksonville, Jewel had only three more stops with Sonny Boy.

The first was to a small house on Lenox Avenue next to Sonny Boy's parents, where the newlyweds lived for about six months and had two horses.

Then, Jewel told Sonny Boy, "Let's live at the farm."

The farm was a ramshackle house built in the 1880s on forty wooded acres off Normandy Boulevard purchased by Sonny Boy with moonshine money for $1,000.

A pig trail dirt road was the only way in and out. There was no electricity or running water.

"We can't move. We ain't got electricity," resisted Sonny Boy.

"I hadn't had nothing all my life so that wasn't no problem for me," said Jewel. "I said, 'I've lived without electricity before.'"

On Sonny Boy's twenty-first birthday in March 1955, the Griffins moved to Diamond D.

In the early days and months at Diamond D, when Jewel would take her children into town, if it rained, she wouldn't be able to get back to the ranch. When that happened, Donnie Wynn, son of Sonny Boy's best friend Donald Wynn, said Jewel and the kids would stay at their house on Crystal Springs Road, "until they could get home."

On their fiftieth wedding anniversary, in 2004, Jewel moved for the final time. It was to what she called her dream house, a log cabin built by Sonny Boy sitting next to a ranch pond.

She and Sonny Boy were married sixty-four years when he passed away January 26, 2018.

## What People Say About Jewel Griffin

### Jodi Coxwell
"I always loved going to Christmas mass with Granny and daddy. That's something we did together. She always was in her Bible. That really humbled me. Granny prayed a lot and a lot of prayer brought us through. She even prays for her boarders."

### Galynna Kittrell Griffin
"If she loves you, she's always going to be there for you. She's going to stand up for you, no matter what. She'll stop whatever she's doing if somebody's in need. Years ago, she encouraged me. When times get bad you had to get up and fight back. You don't just lie down. You make things happen. She's always been like another mother to me."

### Amy Griffin
"Granny has always been there. She's a sweet person. She's a Godly woman. She is always praying, always spiritual. She's always doing the right thing. You can talk to her about everything. She'd give you her advice whether you liked it or not. She was going to tell you what she thinks. She was going to be very honest with you."

### K'Leigh Griffin Combs
"My Granny is just inspirational. She can come across a little rough and tough, and she is. Granny has always been a caretaker her whole life. She took care of her mother-in-law and her father-in-law. She took care of my Big Daddy. She is just a selfless person. It's never about her. It's always about the family."

**Cathy Griffin Melton**

"I learned a lot from my mother. I learned how to take care of a horse, compassion, and love for people and animals. You've got to love what you're doing, and you've got to love the people that you do it with."

**Dr. Tammy Jordan**

"She's a Saint. She might be a little rough around the edges…and some people may be a little scared of her sometimes, too…but she's the most God-fearing person. She will do anything for anybody. She is just the fabric that holds everything together. Dedicated to her family and friends and has a passion for animals."

**Marty Higdon**

"Gran Jewel has got to be one of the toughest women I have ever had the privilege of being around. She's Godly. She prays. She goes to church. She expects you to do what you're supposed to do. Now, on the other hand, she'd whip your ass for just about anything."

**Tiffany Jordan Williamson**

"Granny can be stern. She said how she wanted it done and she wanted it done right then. That's okay. I was like a sponge as a kid, and you learn it. You know how to do it that way and you did that way. When I worked for her, I would try to change things up, and she said, 'Nope. You're going to do it this way.'"

**Jane Wiggins**

"Jewel is like the Rock of Gibraltar. Jewel was the person to figure stuff out. She's quiet, but she's very deep. She's very smart. She's got a lot of insight and she reads people."

**Neni Jenkins**

"She is a giving, caring person. The only other person in the whole world I would give this high credit to would be my mother. Jewel, her nature on the importance of giving and helping other people came from my mother. When you think my mother had thirteen children and she raised them all, you know what a strong person that has to be. That's where I put Sissy on that pedestal."

## Patricia Wright

"Mother is a devout Catholic. She's a good person. She's an honest person to the core. She's a very strong person. Her strength, her goodness. My faith has a lot to do with my mother, and I'm grateful for that."

# THE GENTLE COWBOY GIANT

―――⧜―――

*"Everybody was afraid of daddy. In all reality, he was a gentle giant with as big a heart as anybody. He'd do anything to help anybody. Daddy had a lot of friends. He was a people person."*

(Author's Note: In the process of researching this book, I delighted in listening to many stories about the life and times of Sonny Boy Griffin. Unfortunately, I was unable to hear some of the legendary tales directly from Sonny Boy, himself, because of his passing on January 26, 2018. This chapter is but a morsel. The other chapters help to paint a more complete portrait of this widely loved man).

FROM TIME TO time, a character so extraordinary comes along and it is said the person is, "larger than life."

Sonny Boy Griffin certainly fit that description.

His first four decades on this earth were at times full of hard drinking, ruckus behavior and dare-devil adventures. Bar room brawls were as

*Sonny Boy often used his big fists.*

common to Sonny Boy as riding bucking bulls and saddle broncs, racing stock cars, and brewing illegal moonshine whiskey.

He was also a stern, loving dad to his four children, sharing with them and nine grandchildren his affection for the land, its horses, and cattle, just as he taught them how to hunt deer and turkey.

Along with his wife Jewel, he helped instill in them all an ethic that embraces hard work and demands doing your very best.

"He gave us so much and left so much for us," said son Michael. "Daddy had a schedule, and we all worked the schedule. He spent a lot of time teaching me guns and hunting, cutting and posting wood, building fences, penning cows, bailing hay. Anything to deal with the farm."

Sonny Boy became a successful cattle rancher who started with Cracker cattle on forty acres of hard scrabble land off Normandy Boulevard in Jacksonville's far westside. Today, Diamond D Ranch covers five hundred acres where Michael maintains and grows the ranching tradition with five hundred cows and a horse rental barn. Sonny Boy's widow, Jewel, continues to operate a boarding barn with sixty horses.

"He grew up and all he wanted was to be a cowboy," said Michael.

Sonny Boy started young. As a twelve-year-old he worked with legendary cowboy "Speedy" Solomon on a crew hunting cows in South Georgia near the Okefenokee Swamp.

Solomon became his "Uncle Speedy," cowboy mentor, and a lifelong friend.

"He was a cow man," said Michael. "He knew cattle and he taught that to me. He knew what cows needed, how to take care of cows, how to make a profit with a cow. It's hard to make a profit with a cow. There's an art to it. There's a fine line, no room for waste."

Sometimes, waste occurs naturally, like it did when lightening struck at the ranch during a storm, killing eleven of Michael's cows, four calves, and a bull.

"Big Daddy, Granny Jewel, and my mom and dad rode up to see the devastation," said granddaughter K'Leigh. "There wasn't one of us that didn't have tears in our eyes."

Seeing the dead farm animals, a sad Sonny Boy said, "You've got to own one to lose one."

Born Dewey Franklin Griffin, Jr., on March 7, 1934, he was raised around his father's grocery/butcher shop on Lenox Avenue where he learned to cut meat and make moonshine.

Because of his red hair and constant sunny disposition, his mother tagged him Sonny Boy early in his life. From that day on, he was Sonny Boy to all who knew him.

Growing up, his best friend was Donald Wynn. Two years older than Wynn, Sonny Boy and Donald "hung out at Daddy Griffin's store on Lenox," said Wynn's son, Donnie.

They remained best friends for life. "They hunted together, moonshined together, ran together," said Donnie. "My dad was kind of like his sidekick."

Little was understood about Dyslexia when Sonny Boy was in school. He struggled with his studies and quit school before really learning to read and write. "He didn't learn to read because he saw everything backwards," said Jewel. He left school after the third grade.

His friend Donald often said that Sonny Boy started school two years before him, but he had passed Sonny Boy by the third grade.

"My dad read most of his mail when Jewel didn't."

Just the same, Sonny Boy became an astute businessman who knew how to make deals and count money.

"Daddy wasn't an educated man, but daddy was very smart with numbers," said daughter Cathy.

"He could figure faster than you can figure on a damn computer," said Jewel. "He learned how to figure money from an early age."

He was also shrewd.

When Jewel and Sonny Boy were young, he took her to race their horses, usually against men.

"They'd find a horse and sneak up on the others," said Michael, meaning they'd make sure their superior horse didn't win the race.

"They'd hold the horse up one week and bet a little bit. They'd go back the next week and turn that thing loose and bet a lot. They made a living doing that."

At every opportunity, Sonny Boy would purchase more land for the ranch. "He bought the Bell place that had timber on it," said Michael. "He talked to the timber company and borrowed money to pay for the land. Then, when he sold the timber on the land, he paid off the debt."

Brother-in-law Frank Jenkins learned from personal experience about Sonny Boy's business savvy. "He beat me out of money a couple of times," Jenkins said. "Not stealing, but horse trading. He was a helluva horse trader. I had a herd of cows and was hurting financially and couldn't feed them." Jenkins also didn't have enough pasture to keep them on.

"One day I made a comment that I needed to get rid of them." Sonny Boy sent a truck and trailer to pick them up the next day. "He paid me about three-fourths of what they were worth. Then he took them to the sale and made money on them."

Longtime friend Frank Spencer said Sonny Boy, "was a hustler. He bought and sold land, a horse trader and cow trader, moonshiner. If he talked you into buying, he'd squeeze you. He didn't put no more into buying than he absolutely had to. Even if you was trying to feed your poor, sick mother, he wouldn't give you more than a dollar."

When one of Sonny Boy's cows died, leaving seven small calves, son-in-law Jerry Jordan also experienced Sonny Boy's astute trading ways. "They had lost their momma and you had to feed them with a bottle," said Jerry. He asked Sonny Boy, 'What you gonna do with them calves?'

"You can have them if you want them," said Sonny Boy.

Jordan took the calves and raised them for three months. "I got them off the bottle, and he said he wanted three of them steers back. I said, all right," said Jordan, amused. "I raised his babies up, and then gave him back three of seven."

"He was a great trader, and he'd always get the better deal, whether it was cattle or horses or land," said boarder Margaret Durrett. "I remember when the paper company was selling off land and he knew about it ahead of time and bid on it."

As good as he was at business, as a young man Sonny Boy had a reputation for hard drinking that sometimes ended in bar fights or other skirmishes. While he maintained his standing as a strong minded, independent, and opinionated man, once he stopped drinking the fights also ended.

"Everybody was afraid of daddy," said daughter Tammy Jordan. "In all reality, he was a gentle giant with as big a heart as anybody. He'd do anything to help anybody. Daddy had a lot of friends. He was a people person."

"Big Daddy was a mountain of a man. He was loud because he was hard of hearing," said grandson Marty Higdon. "When I was a kid growing up, his hands were like he could grab your whole head with one hand and pick you up off the ground. Strong as an ox."

Amy Griffin remembers going to Sunday church as a teenager with her uncle. "They found out who I was, and asked me, 'Your grandfather is Sonny Boy Griffin?'"

"Yes sir."

"Oh," the man responded. "I know where you're from. Now that man, he'll kill you if you step a foot on his property. You don't trespass on his property."

Amy was shocked. "We were around him. He seemed hard, but he was really soft."

"I saw a different side of him whenever Jewel and I were doing a cowhide race or something like that and he feared she was going to get hurt," said Jewel's longtime friend Jane Wiggins. "I saw a softer side of him. I figured he wouldn't care. He acted like he was made out of iron or something."

"My Aunt Jewel had a stallion and it bucked him off," said nephew Terry Freeman. "Uncle Sonny Boy took out his pocketknife and gelded him on the spot. He was drunker than a bald owl."

Sonny Boy and Jewel had a pet deer they had raised at Diamond D. Somebody shot it, and the alert went out to family and hunt club buddies to help find the culprit. Aaron Coleman was one of those who responded.

"Sonny Boy went one place and hid, and I got another place."

They spotted a motorcycle and decided to wait on it. "Sonny Boy had been drinking and he was going to shoot whoever it was," said Coleman. "The damn game warden pulled up, riding the motorcycle."

"Don't you ever come back on my property," said Sonny Boy. "I'll kill you if you do."

"If he was out drinking and somebody give him a bunch of crap, you'd better be prepared to defend your honor because he wasn't going to let you get away with it," said nephew Freeman.

Rodney Butler, who's been boarding horses at Diamond D for nearly fifty years, recalled trail riding one day over a spot called Three Bridges, when several men in an SUV drove by. "As they got right up behind me, they stuck the shotgun out the window and fired it."

Butler's horse reared and spun around. "By the Grace of God, I stayed on him."

When Butler returned to the ranch, he told Sonny Boy what had happened.

"I just seen them, and I'm going to talk to them," said Sonny Boy. After a while, Butler said Sonny Boy returned, "with a big grin on his face."

"Well, you ain't got to worry about them today," he said. "They're stuck out there in the sand with a blown axle."

Sonny Boy was also a devilish kidder who, "cut up with everybody," said Michael.

He gave his friends nicknames that were like bumper stickers, staying on for life. Most of the names were useful as CB handles when he and his friends hunted in their trucks.

With nine grandchildren, he always had an audience for his rascal humor.

Tiffany Jordan Williamson would often eat dinner with her grandparents. Once she recalled a jar of homegrown peppers in vinegar. Sonny Boy said, "I betcha can't eat one of them."

"I can eat one faster than you can," she replied, accepting the challenge.

Sonny Boy put a pepper on her dinner plate, then grabbed one for himself. "All right," Sonny Boy said with a smile.

"I took one bite and said, 'Oh my gosh!'" Tiffany finished the pepper but learned a lesson to never take a dare from her Big Daddy.

"He'd play a joke and not even tell you he did it, just to laugh," said granddaughter Jodi Coxwell. After she and David Coxwell were married, Sonny Boy and Donald Wynn, visited the Coxwell retreat in Brooker to fish in the lakes.

"One day, after they left, hogs started showing up and this sow had little piglets." David said, "Your grandpa did that."

"Big Daddy dropped them hogs in there for fun."

In the 1960's, the Beverly Hillbillies was a television sitcom about the Clampetts, a dirt-poor family in the Ozark Mountains who struck oil on their land and became rich. They moved to Beverly Hills to make a new home in a huge mansion.

They had trouble adapting to the ways of Hollywood, including daughter Elly May's collection of non-farm animals.

The show was a favorite of most of America, and it was also must-see television for the Griffin family each week.

Sonny Boy identified with the characters in the cast, but one day he decided something was missing from the show. That's when he and his friend Kenneth Manning caught a live possum, put it in a crate, and shipped it to the show in Los Angeles.

Even though Sonny Boy did it as a prank, apparently the show's producers appreciated the gesture. In July 1963, the Sonny Boy and Kenneth received a letter from Paul Henning, the show's creator and producer. It read in part:

> *"You will be happy to know that he arrived in fine shape and is now living in air-conditioned comfort with some of Elly's 'critters'-six*

*skunks, three racoons, a fox and a squirrel monkey. They have already become fast friends.*

*"In the next week or two we will take a picture of Elly with her one-and-only possum and we will send it to you, autographed by both- if the possum has learned to write by then. It's possible, because Elly's animals board with Mr. Frank Inn, a very famous and wonderful animal trainer.*

*"You may be sure that we will use the possum on the show just as soon as he is camera broke. Thanks from all of us, especially Elly May."*

*Sincerely,*
*Paul Henning*

Sonny Boy was always someone who never hesitated to help his friends and neighbors. In his early seventies he helped someone and it nearly cost him his life.

"He went to a friend's on Yellow Water Road who had a cow having a calf," said Jewel. The cow was having trouble, so Sonny Boy pulled out the calf.

"The next week he got very ill, so on Friday I took him to the emergency room," Jewel recalled. After treating him, Jewel was told to bring Sonny Boy back on Monday. "By the time I got back on Monday his temperature was 105."

When the doctor saw Sonny Boy, he asked him if he had been "messing with cows." Sonny Boy said he had. Because the doctor had interned in Milwaukee, an area known for its milk cows, he told Sonny Boy he had Brucellosis, an infectious disease that people can get when in contact with infected animals like cattle, sheep, goats and pigs.

The doctor said Sonny Boy needed massive doses of Tetracycline, an antibiotic that fights infection caused by bacteria. But first, giving the antibiotic to Sonny Boy required approval from the Center for Disease Control in Atlanta.

Sonny Boy remained in the hospital for three weeks for treatment. "They had to change his bed every couple of hours because he was sweating so much," said Jewel. He lost twenty pounds.

"We were fortunate we had a doctor who was familiar with Brucellosis."

The Griffins have several family traditions that have been handed down from generation to generation. None, over the years has been more important, and more anticipated, than each Easter weekend when most all of the Griffins gather to clean Deese Cemetery, founded by the Deese family in 1911. The cemetery sits on Diamond D Ranch near the log cabin Sonny Boy built for Jewel.

Since Sonny Boy passed away on January 26, 2018, and was buried there on Thursday, February 1, that annual Easter cemetery pilgrimage has taken on a special meeting.

After a day of viewing at Most Holy Redeemer Catholic Church, the family and friends gathered Thursday at 11 a.m. in the Diamond D Pavilion for a celebration of the legacy of Sonny Boy Griffin.

Donnie Wynn, son of Sonny Boy's best friend Donald Wynn, sang Sonny Boy's favorite song, a hymn written by Vince Gill, called "Go Tell It on the Mountain."

The third and fourth verses read:

> "Oh how we cried the day you left us. We gathered around your grave to grieve. I wish I could see the angels faces when they heart your sweet voice sing.

*"Go rest high on that mountain, son, your work on earth is done.*
*Go to heaven a-shoutin' love for the Father and the Son."*

A most meaningful moment in the service came when granddaughter K'Leigh Griffin Combs shared a poem about her Big Daddy that she wrote.

### BIG DADDY'S POEM

We want to hear you tell a story from way back when.
We want to hear you talk about that old cow pen.
We want you to meet a new friend to give them a nickname.
We all know you never gave the same.
He would call it like he saw it,
and if it made you mad well too bad.
A detective Big Daddy should have been,
Cause you couldn't get a thing past him.
He knew everyone's tire track signs,
He knew where you had went & probably even what time.
Oh how we will miss his truck coming by,
As time goes on we'll do our best not to cry.
The sounds of you beepin' that horn at us,
If you could just do it one more time, I promise we would not fuss.
We've spent countless times behind that truck,
Oh what we would do to be behind you once again Stuck.
We will miss your shine in that glass jar,
But your shine will now come from heaven afar.
If only we could ride with you one more time,
And open those gates for you one last time.
We would have liked to have saw your face,
When Jesus opened your last gate.
A Golden heart stopped beating,
Hard at rest.
God broke our hearts to prove to us,
He only takes the best.
So, go ahead bait up those turkey and deer.
Stock up that lake that's somewhere near.

Get some puppies, start training up those hounds.,
We will all be in heaven soon enough to receive our crowns.

**_Written by K'Leigh Griffin Combs_**
**_Inspired by the Grandchildren of_**
**_Sonny Boy Griffin_**

Griffin daughter Dr. Tammy Jordan spoke for the family. Acknowledging those gathered, Dr. Jordan said, "I see some that are friends from his youth and grew up on the westside of Jacksonville with daddy. You may have raced a car with him, ran some moonshine, or drove a few cattle across Jacksonville with him."

She thanked those who were Sonny Boy's hunting pals. "He loved to run those dogs. He would spend from before daylight to dark for those few months of hunting season in the woods."

Dr. Jordan also recognized Sonny Boy's business associates, neighbors and boarders before closing her remarks. "He and momma worked hard to instill in all of us values that would benefit us as we walked through life in our separate directions. He taught us love, respect, hard work ethic, and the love of an animal. He was tough on us when he needed to be but was always there when we needed something.

"He loved his family. I hope you all know how much he loved you. Even in these latter years in life, he was always worrying about how one or the other of us was doing. But that is what daddies do."

It was a service fitting someone who lived a full and memorable life, followed by a procession the short distance to the cemetery, led by a horse drawn carriage.

"When I was a young kid, Sonny Boy was John Wayne," said Donnie Wynn. "He was always there. You think that this ain't supposed to happen. He's supposed to live forever."

## What People Say About Sonny Boy Griffin

### Former mayor John Peyton

"He was an extraordinary guy. He didn't give a rat's ass about what anybody thought about him or anyone else. What you saw is what you got. I got the feeling he had great instincts and he ruled his life by gut instincts. He was well-respected."

### Dwayne Addy

"He was just a down to earth man. He was honest. What he told you, he meant it. It was in stone. If he told you he was going to knock the hell out of you, he meant exactly what he was going to do. He didn't back up."

### Bo Padgett

"He was kind of like a newspaper to me. He knew everything that happened that week, and he'd tell me about it. Then, we'd talk about racing and hot rod cars, and all the stuff they had to do to haul moonshine when they was younger."

### Neni Jenkins

"Have you ever heard the old saying that there's two kinds of farmers? There's one kind that rides around in his truck and raises his hat. There's another kind of farmer that rides around on his tractor and he raises his crop. She's the one that raised the farm. He's the one that raised his hat."

### Jodi Coxwell

"Everybody wanted Big Daddy's dogs, but he would rarely sell them. When he would have extra puppies, he'd sell one. When the dogs got lost sometimes, Big Daddy would say, 'They know their way home. My dogs are smart.' If you couldn't find him, he was at the dog pen, or feeding deer."

### Judge Lance Day

"At first Sonny Boy terrified me. I didn't even know he could walk for a while because he was always in his truck. I remember he snored and when he snored, the whole house shook. He was the loudest snorer I ever heard. And when he snored, he would holler out. We would giggle."

### Donnie Wynn

"Sonny Boy was larger than life. He was a character. No doubt about it. If you ever met him once you remembered him."

### Charles Spencer

"He was the kind of a guy who would push you to the edge just a little farther than someone else. But he was a good man. He loved cattle, and he loved horses."

### Patricia Wright

"Regardless of all the bad things you've heard about my father, he was a wonderful man. He was a good man. He would give you the shirt off his back. I've seen him take in so many people and take care of them."

### Jerry Jordan

"A lot of people talk good about him. He either liked you, or he didn't. I think I kind of grew on him. I was there to take his daughter, and I thought there'd be a little grudge. But he kind of got used to it."

### Margaret Durrett

"Sonny Boy was a character. He had this special humor. It was country special humor. He always made me laugh."

# Two Rough and Tumble Gals Become Fabled Horse Women

*"He went to bulldog the cow, and he ran his horse down the arena. He jumped clear over the steer and landed in the dirt. When he got back, I said, 'Sonny Boy, what do you call that? You didn't even get close to the steer. You jumped clean over him.'" Sonny Boy replied, "Well, I've had too much to drink, Jane. I seen two steers and I jumped on the wrong one."*

JEWEL GRIFFIN AND Jane Wiggins have been best friends for more than seven decades.

It all started when Jane, an 11-year-old with a burning passion for horses, met 14-year-old Jewel Stoddard, someone who shared Jane's hunger for riding. The chance encounter happened at Hyde Park Stables on San Juan Avenue. Jane, a new rider, was getting her very first horse.

"She came riding up to the stables on an Arabian stallion she was training for somebody else," recalled Jane. "She was beautiful, and I thought that was the prettiest horse I'd ever seen." The two became fast friends and constant riding companions, often competing as teammates at rodeos and horse frolics where they won a lot more than they lost.

After 17-year-old Jewel and Sonny Boy married and moved to the small house on Diamond D land, Jane was a constant visitor, and even lived with the young couple for a short time.

"There was a boy, Aaron Coleman, who asked if I wanted to go out there. Aaron borrowed a truck and we put two horses in the back of the truck because you couldn't drive up there. There was just a dirt trail going to the house. Once we got over the cattle gap, we'd unload the horses and ride the rest of the way. That just thrilled me," said Wiggins. The first time she visited the Griffins at Diamond D, "They didn't have electricity. It was exciting."

"I didn't know how to cook a bit, so after I got married, I stayed there with them about six months because my husband went out of town to find us some work," Wiggins recalled. Jewel taught her to cook. In return, Jane did ranch chores, and washed the dishes and dirty laundry.

"A lot of time we'd be eating breakfast, and Sonny Boy would ask me to read the newspaper to him. We did have our arguments," Wiggins said. "It wasn't hostile. I just wanted to be onery."

One day, when Jewel was sick, it fell to Jane to cook breakfast. "I couldn't cook very well at all. I think I poured the grits in the pot before the water boiled, and they wouldn't get done." Sonny Boy asked her, "How long does it take you to make grits? My God." "I said I wasn't a good cook like Jewel, 'so you just sit down and be quiet.'"

But the real friendship between the two women was rooted in their shared love of horses.

"I ran barrels with her, western pleasure stuff. We went to some rodeos," said Jane. "I got interested in showing horses, but I think Jewel found that kind of boring. She didn't like to get in front of people and do stuff. She always liked riding in the woods. We'd get up at 5 o'clock in the morning and go riding in the woods before the kids got up and we had to take them to school."

At one frolic, in the cow pony race Jane rode Sonny Boy's horse, Whiskey. "He had a bad reputation for bucking people off, so I put my brother's thick coat on. A boy told me, 'Jane, if you're going to ride that horse, don't baby him or he'll buck you off.' He said when I get to the starting line, I needed to start whupping his ass. 'Get you a stick and whup his ass. He won't have time to buck because he'll be afraid of you whupping on him.'"

Jewel told Jane, "I don't want you riding that horse. He may hurt you." Wiggins replied, "Sonny Boy done talked me into it. I don't want to be chicken so I'm going to do it." Jane knew if she didn't ride the horse, Sonny Boy would never let her forget it. "He liked to aggravate me, but I like to give it right back to him." Jewel told Jane not to let Sonny Boy scare her. "I'm already scared," she said.

The boy who had told Jane to "whup his ass" gave her a whip and told her to start beating on the horse when she got to the starting line. "Well, I did, and we won, but I was a nervous wreck. I said I was not going to let Sonny Boy talk me into that crap anymore. I had to take the challenge because I didn't want Sonny Boy calling me chicken from then on."

Jewel, riding her yellow horse Apache, finish second.

The two young women were partners in all kinds of joint competitions, including horseback balloon popping. "They would blow up balloons and tie them to your belt loops. You'd ride around popping the other girls' balloons."

Wiggins and Jewel looked out for each other. "We'd say, 'We got to get Martha Ponce because she's winning everything.' So, we popped her balloons first. After that, it was everybody for themselves." Afterwards, Martha Ponce asked if Jane and Jewel were picking on her. Jane said, "Yea. We got to eliminate you so we can win something."

There also was the "handkerchief race," when two riders run side by side holding a handkerchief between them and race around a barrel. "Then you come back as fast as you can. They time you and whoever does the fastest wins," said Jane.

In the "personal pickup" competition, Jewel would run her horse down to the barrel where Jane was waiting on the ground. As Jewel rounded the barrel, Jane would grab the saddle horn and jump up on the rear of Jewel's horse. "One time, Jewel's horse turned real quick to pick me up. It knocked me out cold," remembered Wiggins.

"We were at the sheriff's posse event and Elmer Rudd (westside cowboy and member of the Duval County Road Patrol), run out there and picked me up. He popped me in the back." Rudd raised Jane's arms up, "and he thumped me on the back and knocked the air back into me."

That's when Sonny Boy intervened. "You girls aren't going to do that anymore, I'll tell you that," he said.

The "personal pickup" was not the first or last time Sonny Boy would step in to try and slow down the two fearless female riders.

Perhaps the most frightening and reckless competition of all was the "cowhide race." It was determined that Jane would ride this time since Jewel was riding when the "personal pickup" wreck had happened.

In the "cowhide race," the rider ties a long rope onto a cowhide, then wraps the other end of the rope around the saddle horn. "You race down the arena dragging the cowhide that's flopping around," said Wiggins. When she reached the end of the arena and rounded the barrel, Jewel jumped on the cowhide, grabbed the rope, and held on tight as Jane raced back to the finish line.

"She put on a raincoat so she wouldn't get too dirty," said Jane. "I round the barrel, Jewel jumps on the cowhide and grabs the rope and I drug her back. She ate a lot of dirt, but she didn't get hurt."

Afterwards, Sonny Boy admonished the two women. "You ain't doing that again, either."

Jewel and Jane weren't the only ones riding in horse competitions. Sonny Boy liked to rodeo. "We went to a rodeo in Callahan, and Sonny Boy was going to bulldog. He was pretty pie-eyed," Wiggins recalled. "He went to bulldog the cow and ran his horse down the arena. He jumped clear over the steer and landed in the dirt."

When he got back, Wiggins said, 'Sonny Boy, what do you call that? You didn't even get close to the steer. You jumped clean over him."

Sonny Boy replied, "Well, Jane, I've had too much to drink. I seen two steers and I jumped on the wrong one."

In his younger years, Sonny Boy also enjoyed a well-earned reputation for liking to drink. Often, he'd even share the alcohol with his friends.

"I had this big old dog that somebody dropped off at a gas station. I took him home, Wiggins said. "It was a black dog with curly hair and looked like a poodle crossed with a lab or something. We called him Toby, and Sonny Boy liked him."

After he went to town to buy feed, Sonny Boy often frequented a favorite bar on Normandy Blvd. where he would meet his friends. "He'd take Toby with him, and the dog would go in there with him and sit. They'd take a pie pan and put beer in it and the dog would drink the beer," Wiggins said. After one of the first times Toby went to the bar with Sonny Boy, Wiggins asked him, "Did you get my dog drunk?" "No," said Sonny Boy. "But he sure had a good time."

The last time Wiggins saw Sonny Boy ride in a horse competition, he was relay racing with Jewel, an older man named Col. Irving T. Williams, and Wiggins. "The old man told me I could be the coach," which meant Wiggins went first, then handed off the baton to Sonny Boy, who handed it off to Jewel. Jewel then passed the baton to Col. Williams to finish the race. "We practiced and we won."

In those younger years, Jewel and Jane were constantly challenging each other in friendly competitions.

"We'd always try to do crazy things," said Wiggins.

"One day, we decided we were going to see how high our horses could jump." They got two 55-gallon drums and put a board across the top. "Sonny Boy said we was crazy," Wiggins remembered.

Jewel was riding her prized horse, Murphy. "He was the kind of horse you couldn't take for granted. You could ride him all day and think he's doing good, and about the time you'd pick your leg up, he'd buck you off," said Wiggins.

With Jewel on his back, Murphy jumped the barrels. "I don't believe that," Sonny Boy said.

Jane, on her horse, Dollar, also jumped the barrels. "I said, 'Wow. I can't believe I done that.'"

Sonny Boy was impressed and urged Jane to try the jump again. She took his challenge. "This time, Dollar stopped. I went over the jump, did a flip, and landed on my feet. Sonny Boy said he'd give me ten dollars to do that again."

In her forties, Wiggins started team roping. Jewel, she said, "thought I'd lost my mind."

Jane said her dad always told her when she became 40-years-old, "You got to do something foolish." A friend urged her to learn to rope. "I told him I was 43-years-old, too old to be roping." She turned to legendary cowboy and roper Kenny Williams. "Mr. Kenny said, 'You can ride a horse as good as anybody I know. All you got to do is learn how to swing the rope and place it.'"

Wiggins said, "Okay. Let's do it."

She won a coveted belt buckle her first year of competing. For Wiggins, winning at something new and different reminded Jane of her friend, Jewel. "Jewel always said that if you're going to do something, just do it. She never backed off nothing."

There was much more to Jewel's horse life than riding in rodeos and having fun in the woods. After all, she had a ranch to run that included rental rides and a boarding barn to manage.

"We was cow hunting one time. Sonny Boy was hollering, just trying to round up cattle." Sonny Boy had built a makeshift corral out of cypress limbs. "We are driving the cows in there, and all of a sudden, they take off running. He hollered at us, 'Hurry, cut 'em off. Go to the right.'"

Jewel was running her paint horse, Spot, when he stepped in a hole and fell. "Jewel went flying off and I went to her. The heck with them cows. I asked her if she was okay." Sonny Boy "went to fussing at me." Jane said, "She could have broke her neck or something," I said.

"Jewel's tougher than we think," said Sonny Boy. "You're an ass," Jane shot back. Jewel said she was okay. "Go ahead," she said.

One day, riders from the rental stable failed to return on time, causing Jewel and Jane to worry about their whereabouts. "We thought they got lost, or they stole the horses." The Cecil Field Naval base neighbored Diamond D and the Jennings Forest. "Somehow we got hold of somebody at Cecil Field and they brought a helicopter out there to the stables."

Jewel and Jane climbed into the helicopter to look for the lost riders. "They went riding around where the woods are, and they found those riders." The helicopter pilot landed in a clearing in the woods. "They picked up the riders and Jewel and I rode home with the horses." Worried that they, too, were lost on the journey home, Jane said, "I don't know where I'm at. Do you?" Jewel said, "Yes, I'll get you home."

There was also fun to be had by the two women that had nothing to do with horses.

One day, Wiggins' husband traded one of their horses for a funeral hearse. Jane commandeered the hearse so Jewel and she, both in their early twenties, could ride it around Jacksonville. Toby, the beer-sipping black dog, rode in the back where the coffin was kept.

Wiggins did the driving. "One day we went by the Normandy Cemetery and people thought we were leading a procession. They pulled over," Wiggins remembered. Jewel said, "Oh no. I don't want anybody to see me." She slid down in the seat. "I thought it was funny."

On another occasion, Jewel and Jane loaded up all the kids in the hearse and drove to the Normandy drive-in to watch a movie.

# YOUNG RURAL PIONEERS
# TO BIG TIME RANCHERS

*"Horses are a luxury and people just left their
horses here. We had to sell a lot of horses and we
went from 86 horses to about 40 horses."*

ON MARCH 7, 1955, Jewel and Sonny Boy Griffin, a young, newly married couple, began their pioneering life on 40 acres in west Jacksonville. Ever since, Diamond D Ranch has been a working ranch.

The land was purchased by Sonny Boy's father, Dewey Griffin, Sr., a full-time butcher and successful moonshiner. The 40 acres were bought with moonshine profits, a business that Sonny Boy and Jewel would continue at Diamond D during their first hard scrabble years there.

"It was Diamond D when I moved out here with my husband," said Jewel, recalling that the couple, both teenagers, were married 13 months earlier, in January 1954. They moved on Sonny Boy's twentieth birthday.

The first Diamond D brand appeared on the door of Sonny Boy's pickup truck, promoting Diamond D Training Stables.

When they married, the young Griffins lived near his father's grocery on Lenox Avenue. "I was the one who wanted to move out here, not Sonny Boy," said Jewel. "I was tired of living next door (to the in-laws)."

The ranch was mostly raw land, reachable only by negotiating a pig trail of a road, best done on horseback. When Sonny Boy told Jewel the property had no power or running water, she didn't care. "I told him I'd been without electricity before."

Only an old log shack, built as a goat farm in the 1880s, stood on the land. A one-armed Black man lived in the house with his goats.

"We scrubbed and we scrubbed," said Jewel in an effort to make the house livable. "Our only partitions was cardboard boxes."

There were roaches everywhere, she said. "It was crawling with roaches in between the logs. We sprayed and sprayed."

The house had two small bedrooms, "and a lean-to kitchen," where Jewel cooked meals on a gasoline stove and kept food in a gasoline powered refrigerator.

Before they finally got electricity, the Griffins drilled a well with a hand pump. Later they added a gas pump.

Jewel's longtime friend Jane Wiggins will never forget her first visit to Diamond D. "There were woods and a crummy dirt road," she said. "It was real basic. They had this house that was kind of crummy. The heater was a wood stove. They were living rough, and I said, how do you do this?"

Sonny Boy's father got the couple yellow paint from a company that painted railroad cars. "In those days we didn't know anything about lead paint. We painted everything," said Jewel.

At the time, Sonny Boy was hanging sheet rock for a company in town. The men who ran the company offered him a deal. "His boss told him if Sonny Boy would throw them a barbecue, they would sheet rock the house. We fixed them up some hogs," said Jewel.

Sonny Boy and Jewel then added new windows.

The closest electricity to Diamond D was on Normandy Blvd., two miles away. After living eighteen months without electric power, the electric company said, "They would run electricity near us, and whether we used it or not, we had to pay $27 a month."

Jewel's dad, Jack Stoddard, was considered a "Jack of all trades." He wired the house for electricity.

When the Griffins sold cows, they continued to fix their house.

Being a cattle rancher can be hard, even on the best of days. It was especially tough on the young Griffins and other cattle ranchers across the country when the feared screwworm flies invaded their pastures and infected the cows, especially newly born calves.

The screwworm fly larvae feeds on the living tissue of warm-blooded animals.

"We had to ride the range when the cows had their calves, rope the calf and doctor it with screwworm medicine," recalled Jewel. The medicine, she said, "was black stuff that looked like tar." The medicine was in a can that had a spout, and it was squirted onto the calf's naval cord to keep the flies from getting in to lay their eggs. "If the fly gets in the naval it kills the calf." A paste was put over the tar-like medicine after it was applied to the naval cord.

Before they were eradicated, screwworm flies caused great financial stress to many ranches, including Diamond D.

Over those early years, the Griffins raised and sold cows, hogs and moonshine. Sonny Boy took jobs for other people, penning their cows for extra money. "He knew how to make money," Jewel said of Sonny Boy. Often, they used their profits to purchase more and more land.

In 1960, six years after they moved to Diamond D, Jewel opened her horse rental barn. She had six horses and six stalls. She charged $1.50 an hour to rent a horse.

*Ranchers Sonny Boy and Jewel take are break.*

"It just grew and grew." The only help she had were her children and their friends who worked after school and on weekends. No one was paid.

"I did whatever had to be done. Nobody helped me," she said. "Sonny Boy was hanging sheet rock and a man hauling hay came up and said his truck was broke down. He told me he would give me the hay if we unloaded it. I unloaded the whole trailer of 300 bales."

Despite the stress of running a ranch, Jewel and Sonny Boy always had time to do things with her children, especially when it involved cows and horses. Daughter Tammy Jordan says her fondest memories as a child at Diamond D was showing cattle. "It was the one activity that I participated in that both daddy and momma were a big part of."

She showed beef and dairy cattle throughout her teenage years, normally placing in the shows. "It was a natural extension of my life on the farm at Diamond D, and with my hard work and the expertise and knowledge of the best cattleman in the county, there was no excuse but to do well."

Jewel, she said, "was my taxi. She made sure with all the other duties she had on her plate that she got me to every cow show. It didn't matter where it was."

One day, after coming home from a long-distance endurance competition, Jewel discovered that her 38-stall rental barn had burned to the ground. "That's when I quit renting horses."

Her son, Michael, and his wife Galynna would reopen and expand the rental stables.

Sonny Boy and Jewel then built a boarding barn, something Jewel said she'd dreamed about "all my life."

The first boarding barn had 24 stalls. "It filled up rapidly," said Jewel. Eventually, Diamond D's boarding barns contained 86 stalls and were "full of horses. We had a waiting list of ten or more people all the time," she said.

When the recession hit the United States in 2007-2009, Jewel's boarding business suffered. "Horses are a luxury and people just left their horses here," she said. "We had to sell a lot of horses and we went from 86 horses to about 40 horses."

One hot summer day during that period, Jewel's mother visited her at the barn. "I was exhausted." As a child, Jewel had prayed for horses. But on this day, she asked her mother, "How do you unpray horses?"

Today, the Diamond D's two boarding barns are full, housing over fifty horses. Boarders pay monthly for their horses to have hay, feed, and turnout daily. The stalls are cleaned five days a week, and riders have use of the two tack rooms.

The Griffin's daughter, Tammy, is the barn veterinarian, and she lives on the ranch. Jewel's younger sister, Joy Harmon, helps her run the barn operation. Joy lives in the original house adjacent to the boarding barns.

Jewel and her boarders, many who've kept their horses there for years, share a special bond. "I love my boarders. I treat them like family, and they feel like they are family," she said.

Eighty-year-old Rodney Butler started making regular trips to Diamond D in 1976 when he was brought there by his father, who boarded his horse at Diamond D and rode in the woods. "I haven't missed many weeks since," he said.

"Dad asked Mrs. Griffin if she had some kind of horse he could buy for me so I could ride with him. It just so happened she had a paint horse with a saddle, bridle, and everything ready to go."

Butler's father passed away in 1980. He continues to come out to the ranch about three times a week to ride with his daughter.

"They're like family, all of them. They've been so good to me. It's the highlight of my life," said Butler. The Griffins, he said, "love the horses and love the ranch. They love to see people happy. If you weren't happy, you were told you might not be in the right place. There's always harmony in this place."

When Butler's horse colicked "and swole up as big as a cow," Jewel stayed up with him all night while he walked the horse. "She knew it was really bothering me, and she knew the horse was going to die."

Around 7 a.m., Butler said Jewel told him to go home. "We can take care of it," Jewel said. "She's that kind of person."

Margaret Durrett grew up in England. When she relocated to Jacksonville from Texas, she moved into the Mandarin community on the city's southside, about a 45-minute drive from Diamond D.

Durrett has been boarding at Diamond D since 1993. After she settled into Mandarin, she started looking for a barn to board her horse. Durrett found that most boarding operations had only stalls and corrals, with no pastures. Diamond D, she said, "was a place that had a pasture, and the horses could be more like a horse."

She said a friend of hers sometimes asks why she goes that far to board at Diamond D when there are stables much closer to where she lives. She responds, "This is personal. Everybody knows everybody. Everybody helps everybody. I say to my husband, 'You can pay a shrink, or you can pay for my horse.'"

Twenty-five years ago, when Durrett's horse got too old to ride, Jewel suggested she buy a horse already at the barn that was for sale. "I've had him since he was seven and now, he's thirty-two. Obviously, he's the horse for me."

Durrett said she believes in fate, and thinks it was fate that brought her to Diamond D twenty-eight years ago. "I think we're all destined to do things, and I think this is where I was supposed to be. Jewel is like a second mother to me, even though we don't have that much age difference between us."

In December 2004, fifty years after they first moved into the original dilapidated log house, Jewel and Sonny Boy moved into what she called her, "dream house," a beautiful new log cabin on the lake.

During her trips to North Carolina for endurance competitions, Jewel saw many log homes, and decided she wanted one. Sonny Boy sold ten acres of property in Lake City to finance the construction. It was his fiftieth wedding anniversary gift to Jewel.

One day riding through the woods, Stewart Dowless, a hunting friend, asked Sonny Boy, "Why did you build that nice house?"

"Well, Stewart, I'll tell you. Jewel was riding that horse, and when it threw her and her head swelled up like a foot tub, I thought we was going to lose her. It worried me to death. As soon as she got well, I decided to build this house because she'd wanted it for some time."

To make the big move into a new home, Jewel needed to have someone competent to live in the log house adjacent to the barn and become her around the clock barn manager. She wanted someone who would follow her instructions and maintain great relationships with all the boarders.

She turned to her friend and riding companion, Pamela Dwyer, a schoolteacher, and new mother. As Jewel and Sonny Boy moved out of the original house into their new log cabin, Pamela, her husband and their child moved in.

# Make Pulpwood or
# Make Whiskey.

———— ❧❧ ————

*"They told Jewel to be quiet. Sonny Boy was driving*
*in and she knew they were going to catch him because*
*there was sugar and stuff they needed for that still in*
*the truck. They told her, 'Now you be quiet.' They were*
*going to arrest him when he came into the house."*

BEFORE, DURING AND after the Great Depression, most of the southern states had their share of illegal family moonshine operations. The federal government once estimated there were at least 10,000 stills nationwide.

Northeast Florida and West Jacksonville were no exceptions.

Stills were hidden in the Westside woods and near many of the creeks in Jennings Forest. Neighboring Baker County had so many moonshine operations it earned the reputation as Shine Capital of the South.

In the beginning, most folks who made and sold moonshine did so as a way to survive financially. These were God-fearing, hard working farm families who tended cows and hogs and planted crops during the day, then retreated into the darkness deep in the woods at night to brew their shine.

To make a living, Jewel Griffin recalls, "You either made pulpwood or you make liquor. And pulp wooding was too damn hard."

Her husband, Sonny Boy, started making and hauling moonshine as a boy. In the March 2017 issue of The Florida Cattleman, Sonny Boy said, "Back when I was young, that's the only way you can make a living. Either that or pulpwood, and I was too sorry to pulpwood."

After World War II, making and distributing illegal "white lightning" became more lucrative, allowing its brewers to sock away cash and buy property. It also became far more competitive. And, as state and federal agents began to tighten their nets to arrest moonshiners and destroy their stills, many families left moonshining behind.

Despite the changing landscape, still operations remained secreted away all across Northeast Florida. In 1953, a state beverage agent reported 241 stills in the Jacksonville district.

"Whippoorwill" was the theme song in the 1958 movie, "Thunder Road," which told the story of moonshining in Appalachia. Its lyrics sing of a rich truth.

> *"Oh, let me tell the story, I can tell it all. About the Whippoorwill who ran illegal alcohol. His daddy made the whiskey, the son he drove the load, and when his engine roared, they called the highway 'Thunder Road.'"*

Making moonshine was generational as fathers taught their sons. It was also often a family affair as wives, daughters, brothers, and cousins pitched in to help.

The Griffin and Stoddard families who lived in west Jacksonville were deep into moonshining. It all started with Sonny Boy's father, Dewey Griffin Sr., who owned a meat market on Lenox Avenue and discovered that if he could make and distribute shine out of the store, it would give his family a nice financial boost.

"Sonny Boy started moonshining when he was probably 15," said Jewel. He began hauling liquor before he was old enough to have a driver's license. It was something he would continue until the early 1970s, according to nephew Terry Freeman.

Sonny Boy's dad, Dewey, got his start on the first farm he owned in Sanderson, Fl. "He got hooked with the people buying and distributing moonshine around Duval County," said Freeman, who many consider the Griffin family historian.

"He was known for making extremely good moonshine," said Freeman. "He didn't cut corners. He wanted to make sure if it had his name on it, it was a good product. People didn't have to worry about buying something bad from him."

Daddy Griffin had a successful shine operation from his Lenox Avenue meat market. But like so many other illegal brewers, eventually he got caught and spent about six months in a Tallahassee federal prison. When he was released, Dewey Griffin promised, "he wouldn't make and sell moonshine anymore," according to Freeman.

Young Sonny Boy learned how to make good shine early, but he also played a valuable role as a "transporter," or moonshine distributor, even before he was old enough to have a driver's license. Usually, the moonshine was hauled to its distribution point late at night when the roads would be clear of other cars, and safer if there was a chase.

*Sonny Boy (right) learned how to run from revenuers by racing stock cars*

At first, Sonny Boy transported illegal whiskey in a 1940 Ford Coupe, then he got a ton-and-a-half truck that he would load with 100 five-gallon jugs of moonshine, according to The Florida Cattleman. The whiskey was concealed with stacks of lumber, and Sonny Boy also loaded his horse in the back of the truck as a disguise.

"I'd put on my cowboy hat, wave to everybody, and bring moonshine into Jacksonville," he told The Florida Cattleman.

It was a job that took great skills and a lot of courage. You were driving for your livelihood, and often, you were running for your life. In the movie, "Thunder Road," the federal agent played by Gene Barry called shine transporters like Sonny Boy, "wild-blooded and death foolish."

Sonny Boy applied his driving skills as a transporter to stock car racing, and vice versa.

"Sonny Boy was running liquor and he was hauling it to my mother," said his friend, Frank Spencer. "We lived on Park Street and there was a little old cabin behind our house in the woods. That's where they'd put the liquor."

When Sonny Boy and Spencer weren't busy as teenagers doing other things, "We'd run whiskey. It didn't matter whether you had a driver's license or not. If you got caught, they'd put you under the jail."

Once Jewel Stoddard married Sonny Boy Griffin, her family also became involved in the moonshine business. "They needed some help," said Jewel, so Sonny Boy brought them in.

Sonny Boy was such a skilled driver as a transporter, he had a reputation for never being caught by the revenuers. "They couldn't catch him. He always had a pretty good car," said Spencer.

But he came close. Jewel remembers one occasion, shortly after they moved to the little rundown cabin at Diamond D Ranch.

"That house had a porch that went around three sides," she said. "We had a still behind the house, beyond where the gelding pasture is now. My brother was running it."

Jewel was inside the house with her mother and father, who had just arrived with a car full of ten-pound bags of sugar for the moonshine. Sonny Boy pulled up in the yard in front of the house. "They had my brother handcuffed to the tractor. They were standing behind the tractor, and my brother had his hands in the air."

Sonny Boy drove up to the house, then he threw his truck into reverse and took off. According to reports, a local revenue agent, Floyd Bennett, jumped on the truck's hood, confident he'd finally caught Sonny Boy.

Sonny Boy and Jewel had just put up a new fence around the yard. "Sonny Boy hit that fence with that truck and the revenuer tried to grab the mirror of the truck. Sonny Boy hit that fence and hauled buggy," she recalled.

"It liked to have killed him," Sonny Boy said of the revenuer.

"These woods were full of tall trees, and it was easy to hide. He lost them in the trees," said Jewel.

Fortunately for Sonny Boy, his friend, A.M. Burris, had a Ford truck that looked like his. He lived on Normandy Blvd. near Diamond D. "They seen his truck on the road and took his tag number," Jewel said. "They come to arrest Sonny Boy because they thought they had his tag number.

"That's not my tag number," Sonny Boy told the revenuers, most likely with a glint in his eyes. His case was thrown out of court.

On another occasion, Jewel said a revenuer showed up at the house. He asked three-year-old Patricia if her daddy was home. "No, he's at the still," she replied.

For the Griffins, making shine was not a sophisticated operation. In fact, it was often about as basic as it could be, held together with creativity and perseverance.

"We had a still down there at a little creek where we made whiskey," said Jewel. "We'd use the creek water."

Once, when Jewel was pregnant, she taught one of her horses to lay down in the house. "I'd put two fifty-pound bags of sugar on him, then I'd get up behind and ride him to the still with the sugar." When sugar was off loaded, "they would throw five-gallon jugs of whiskey across the saddle, and I would bring the whiskey back to the barn."

For another still that was located in a different secluded spot at Diamond D, Jewel recruited an ox to haul supplies. "They would load all of the makings on a cart and drive the ox to the still to recharge it," she said. Once unloaded, "he'd go back to the barn by himself. He knew that feed was waiting on him."

Jewel's younger sister, Joy Harmon, remembers well when her parents, the Stoddards, operated a still in the woods near their house. "My daddy and brothers dug a tunnel under our house. Daddy tunneled it all the way back to the woods," she said. A large fan was placed at one end of the tunnel to blow any odor out into the woods.

"They had a trap door under my bed where they stored the whiskey. On the nights they came to pick the moonshine up, I had to move out of my room," Joy said. When the trap door was opened, "there would be an assembly line passing them glass jugs up and putting them in these paneled trucks."

One night when Sonny Boy was hauling a paneled truck full of whiskey down Blanding Blvd. one of the truck's doors flew open. "These glass jugs busted all over the highway."

Her father, Joy said, insisted the glass jugs were thoroughly cleaned regularly. "My brother was going to make sure they were cleaned once. We put bleach in a jug and then we put in ammonia. When he put that ammonia in there that jug blew up and it went everywhere," Joy said.

Some of Sonny Boy's pals also made money from moonshine operations. One, Charles Spencer, served as a lookout for a still operator.

"A man made whiskey out in our back pastures," Spencer recalled. "He would come by and get me, and he'd give me $10 to load my horse in in the back of my truck. I would ride the horse around and around out in his whiskey field in case the revenuers showed up."

If revenuers came, Spencer had a plan to warn the moonshiner. "I was sitting up on that horse and I could see the car lights at night. If I saw lights coming, I hollered three times. It means they was breaking through the woods, and he should get out of there."

Once, 17-year-old Spencer and his brother Frank found a still revenuers had destroyed out in the woods. "We got a welder friend of ours and got it fixed. Then we did everything we could to get enough money to buy the corn mash and the sugar. We set us up and we was going to get rich. It was a big whiskey still." The brothers put the still on their grandfather's land.

The Spencer brothers dreams of new wealth didn't last long. Revenuers discovered the rebuilt still. A hose they were using to run water from their grandfather's well to the still, "had been chopped every foot for a quarter of a mile. They chopped that whiskey still all to pieces this time. You couldn't glue it back together."

However, the revenuers, never touched his grandfather's well. "I said they know exactly who I am. They don't have to worry about me. I'm not going to make no more moonshine."

Sonny Boy's younger hunting buddy, Dwayne Addy, remembers when he was a kid that his dad, Sonny Boy, and a friend named Billy Coleman, "had a still back there at the old hog place where I grew up behind Herlong Airfield."

Even as a boy, Dwayne was involved in the operation. "They had an old sled and pulled it through the swamp to where they was back there cooking. When they'd make a sugar run, I'd get on the horse and take the sugar back there to them. Then daddy would always make me go home."

# This Acorn Didn't Fall
# Far From the Tree

———❦———

*"I'll never forget one time I left the door to the feed room open, and the cows got in. They made a mess. He sent me out there to clean it up. I was talking to myself, and I was talking bad about him. He come up in that room where I was at, and I stood up and he slapped the hell out of me."*

*"Now, clean it up."*

**THERE'S AN OLD** saying most of us first heard as children. "Usually, an acorn doesn't fall far from the tree."

Certainly, that is true of Michael Griffin, the only son of Jewel and Sonny Boy Griffin.

On the one hand, family members and friends describe Michael as tough and sometimes hot-headed like his dad. "When he gets mad his daddy comes out," said Michael's wife Galynna. "You don't push Michael. When you push Michael into a corner, he's gonna come out fighting."

His sister, Dr. Tammy Griffin, said they are similar in another way. "Michael and daddy are a lot alike, reaching out to people, doing things with a big heart, doing things for people."

Some say his kindness and strong faith is very much like his mother. "He loves the Lord and he's a good man," said Galynna. "He is very compassionate like his mother. If he thinks somebody needs something, they don't have to tell Michael."

And like both of his parents, Michael mirrors the Griffin's commitment to hard work and dedication to the family.

"It's never ending on a farm, feeding and tending to the animals, fence work," said Galynna. "Michael is the hardest working man I know, starting before daylight and working until way after dark."

"When we got home from school, we had a job," Michael said. "We cleaned horse stalls and we baled a lot of hay."

Michael and his three sisters, he said, "have a lot of respect for mom and dad, and the reason we do is because we watched how hard they worked all their lives."

Summer vacations were extremely rare. "We didn't take them, didn't do it. When it came that time of the year and everybody was at the lakes and rivers, you would bale hay."

Michael does remember a rare trip to Disney World right after the theme park opened in Orlando. "Momma took us when we was kids. It was a day trip. Down there and back. We didn't go nowhere. Everything was here."

Recreation for the Griffin kids was camping out at the creek on the ranch, fishing, hunting and riding horses. "We'd get on those horses and ride every step of these woods."

While riding horses was great fun, it also came with some risks, especially for a young, rambunctious boy.

As a six-year-old, Michael was riding barefoot on his pony, Pinocchio, when the pony ran up on the back of another horse, causing it to kick back toward Michael and hit him on his foot. The blow knocked off his big toe.

"The doctors tried to sew it back on, but after a while it went to smelling," said Jewel, Michael's mother. She took him back to the doctor. "The doctor asked me if I was strong," she recalled. "I said I was strong." But when the wrapping was removed and Michael's sewed on toe fell to the floor, so did Jewel. "I fainted."

To try and save the toe, the doctors grafted the toe bone onto Michael's calf. He stayed in Hope Haven Hospital the rest of the summer with his leg in a sling. "It grew back with the toenail," said Jewel.

Sonny Boy and Jewel always had a garden that supplied the family with vegetables. "The prettiest garden you ever seen," said Michael. "Me and my sisters rowed that thing. There wasn't a weed. I hated that damn garden."

Every night, he said the family shelled peas and shucked corn while watching television.

The Griffins didn't eat meals away from the ranch. "Momma cooked every meal, and it was a meal," he said. "A breakfast would cover a table. She always claimed she wasn't much of a cook, but to me she was the best cook because she fried food and made gravy."

Another way people say Michael is like Sonny Boy is their shared love for cows. It all began as work when Michael was a child. "He was a cowman. He knew cattle and he taught that to me," he said.

"I rode cattle with my daddy in the woods, and sewed wounds in cows," he said. Michael explained that when a cow has a calf too large, the cow will prolapse, meaning the cow's tissues that normally are a tube inside the body turn inside out and bulge from the body.

Michael and his dad covered the wound with sugar, which would shrink the wound to about the size of a baseball. "We'd push it back and sew up the vagina, then turn her loose. The wound would heal, and the next time she would come in the cow pen, daddy would sell her."

Jewel finished eleventh grade, and Sonny Boy left school after the third. Michael said, "They was real particular about the grades we made in school. I wasn't no straight A student, but you didn't make Ds and bring them home to our house. Anytime we had trouble, momma would sit right there with us."

Sonny Boy held rodeos at Diamond D and many other places. Michael said he maintained bucking bulls and broncs and roping steers. "Daddy rode saddle broncs. He liked to show off. He was good at what he done."

As a teenager, Michael developed Sonny Boy's love for rodeoing. He also liked playing football, but he learned quickly from his dad he couldn't do both.

"I was playing football and I made the team. The coach really wanted me to play," he recalled. "About that time, I started rodeoing and I got pretty good at it, and I wanted to rodeo." Michael was going to high school rodeos that were held most every weekend, and usually a good distance from Diamond D.

When it became time for spring football training at Baldwin High School, Michael made the team. He was planning to return to the team after the summer to play for the season. "Daddy told me I was going to have to make a decision. 'You're going to rodeo or play ball. I don't care which one.'"

Michael chose rodeo, but when he told his football coach, the coach wasn't happy. "He went on and on about it." The coach gave Michael a ride home so he could speak with Sonny Boy.

"I want that boy to play football," the coach told Sonny Boy.

"Well, that's the boy's decision," answered Sonny Boy.

"He said you weren't going to let him play."

"Well, he told you wrong. I told him to make a choice, and it was his choice," said Sonny Boy.

Like soccer moms today, Jewel was a rodeo mom, hauling Michael every weekend to a rodeo so he could compete. "Man, momma hauled me all over the country."

It was important for one of his parents to remain at the ranch while the other was away, Michael said. Jewel drove to rodeos that required long travel, in part because Sonny Boy had difficulty reading road signs. That meant that his dad only got to watch Michael rodeo when an event was held in nearby places like Hilliard or Callahan.

While Sonny Boy had a well-earned reputation for his toughness, Jewel was more the family disciplinarian. But Michael's dad did have his moments.

"I'll never forget one time I left the door to the feed room open, and the cows got in. They made a mess. He sent me out there to clean it up."

Michael was not happy. "I was talking to myself, and I was talking bad about him," he said. "He come up in that room where I was at, and I stood up and he slapped the hell out of me."

"Now, clean it up."

Michael said he doesn't remember many whippings from his dad, "but you knew he would."

On the other hand, his mother was known by her children and other kids who hung out at Diamond D as someone with a firm hand who didn't tolerate nonsense, talking back or acting up.

"I was twelve or thirteen-years-old and I'd done something wrong," said Michael. "She was whipping me." Young Michael then magnified the reason for his discipline. "I turned around and was laughing at her."

Without hesitation, Jewel responded. "She hit me in the face with that belt. I didn't laugh no more."

Sometimes, when he and his buddies would break one of his mother's rules, they got lucky. "Me and Michael took a horse swimming one time, and if she had caught us...," said friend Bo Padgett. "We actually only took one horse in a pond. We was going to have us a rodeo."

Michael rode his horse out into the pond. "I was going to slip up on the horse's back, grab it by the flank, and get it to buck. We knew it couldn't hurt us out there in the water," said Bo.

The horse wasn't going to cooperate. "It thought something was in the water like a gator and it went nuts."

When the two twelve-year-old boys got off the horse, "It just sunk. Bubbles went to coming up, and we thought we'd killed one of Jewel's rental horses."

The boys, in neck high water, started feeling around for the horse. "About that time, it come up. It just lunged out of there and it was blowing water out of both nostrils. It almost landed on top of us." Then, the horse went under water again.

"It made one more of those lunges coming out, and we got hold of the reins and got it out of the water."

Bo said Michael kept saying, "Momma's gonna kill us."

Fortunately for the two boys, the horse didn't drown, and it was raining hard that day. "That was our excuse for the saddle and everything being wet."

While he worked hard at the ranch, passed his classes in school and won belt buckles rodeoing, Michael, like a lot of teenage boys in those years, had his rebellious side. Having long hair was one way for him to show it.

As a junior at Baldwin High School, a chance meeting at the Valentine's Day prom was a turning point in his life, including getting his hair cut. That's when he met fifteen-year-old Galynna Kittrell, the daughter of Sonny Boy's arch enemy, Jim Kittrell.

Michael and Galynna were married while still in high school. They moved into a two-bedroom mobile home at Diamond D.

Michael finished high school, but his mother missed his graduation.

"I was thirty-seven-years-old, and I had cervical cancer," recalled Jewel.

"I had to have surgery and it was scheduled the same week of Michael's graduation."

She asked her doctor if the surgery could be delayed a week so she could see Michael graduate. "He was a cancer doctor, and he knew something had to be done right away. He said, 'I don't care who's graduating. This is more important than any graduation.'"

# BUTCHERING MEAT: FAMILY TRADITION AND A SCIENCE

*"They'd get in there and ground the beef up and ground the sausage. You could hear the machines. I remember doing this from when I was in diapers walking around until I think I was fifteen. That's what I miss the most."*

**DEWEY GRIFFIN, SR.,** the family patriarch, owned Griffin's Grocery on Lenox Avenue where he butchered cows he raised between Marietta and Whitehouse, then sold the meat to his many faithful customers.

By all accounts, Dewey Griffin was an excellent butcher who made moonshine at his store equally as well.

As a boy growing up, Sonny Boy Griffin learned from is dad how to butcher meat, a skill he later taught his own son, Michael Griffin.

The Griffin family is loaded with traditions that have lasted and been passed down for decades. Perhaps none is more memorable for at least four generations of Griffins than butchering cows, hogs, goats and deer at Diamond D.

If you are a member of the Griffin family under the age of ninety, odds are great you've participated in butchering and processing meat at Diamond D.

"Daddy Griffin bought a mobile home and moved out here," said Michael. "Every July 4th, Labor Day, Memorial Day, Christmas and New Year's, he had a lot of Black customers who would want a pig dressed fifty pounds, cleaned and gutted and hung in the cooler. They would also want a goat or two."

Over the years, the Griffins also cut and wrapped meat for their Diamond D Ranch neighbors and customers. "We had a walk-in cooler and we butchered for other people," said Jewel. "We usually didn't butcher our cows and sell the meat, but we butchered other people's beef for them."

Everybody, Jewel said, "had a job." That included family members who wrapped the meat and wrote what was inside on the wrapping paper. "Afterwards, we'd put it back in the cooler and call the people to come get it."

Like all of the Griffin grandchildren, Amy Griffin said butchering, processing, and packaging meat on the ranch was an event she looked forward to. "We'd work cows and then we'd come back, and they would kill how many they were going to butcher," said Amy.

The cows would be butchered at Sonny Boy's dog pen. "When he growed up Big Daddy was butchering meat all the time," said oldest grandson Marty Higdon. "He could grab a 300-pound quarter cow out of the cooler with one arm and bear hug that thing, walk out the door, and shut the cooler, put the cow down on the table in the meat shed, and go to cutting on it."

Once the meat was butchered, it was transported to the boarding barn near the ranch entrance for processing and packaging.

"They'd get in there and ground the beef up and ground the sausage. You could hear the machines. I remember doing this from when I was in diapers walking around until I think I was fifteen," said Amy. "That's what I miss the most."

When the work was done, Jewel took over, cooking fresh hamburgers for lunch and steaks for supper. "We always had a steak off a cow we cut," said Jewel.

Butchering at Diamond D was a strenuous, well-planned happening, not simply cutting up some meat at holidays.

For instance, the Griffins and their friends would catch hogs in the woods while the hogs were feeding. "We'd cut their ears, cut their tails and castrate them," said Michael. Once the hogs were castrated, they were called, "bar hogs."

The bar hogs would then be released. A year later, the hogs that had been cut would be caught again for butchering. "They would dress fifty pounds and be a perfect little pig."

The Griffins would then put the newly caught bar hogs in a pen on the ranch and feed them for two months. The next step, said Michael, was to "kill them."

The hogs were then scalded, and their hair was peeled off by hand. "I was a scalder more than a butcher," said Marty Higdon. "I could also cut them and help put them in the cooler. I was still a little fella."

After the hog was scalded and its hair removed, "He'd be just as pretty and clean," Michael said. Next was removing the hog's guts. "Daddy did it with his hands."

Michael describes cow butchering like it is a science that must be done the right way for the best results. "When you buy a steak at the grocery, it's usually only three days old. They killed it, trucked it, and the meat cutter cut it."

But not at Diamond D.

"We'd kill a steer and hang it in the cooler for at least seven days," he said.

During those seven days, the blood and liquid in the joints drips out slowly onto shavings spread out on the walk-in cooler floor to help flavor the meat. "The shavings would draw the liquids out of the meat and then get back into the air and back into the meat. The sawdust would keep the air dry."

After the butchering, the freshly cut meat was loaded into a truck and taken into the Griffin house where it was laid out on the dining room table, wrapped, and identified.

Once all the butchering, processing, and packaging was finished, cleaning up was tackled with the same teamwork and intensity. "They were so clean and neat. You didn't get more thorough cleaning the meat grinders and the saws. It was so impressive," said Michael.

Eventually, Michael said the butchering operation at the ranch grew so large it became too much to continue with all of the other demanding ranch work. "We did four or five hogs a week, and a cow a week."

Today, Michael continues to use the butchering skills handed down from his grandfather and father, but only on a limited basis, and mostly on special occasions.

# Riding, Working, No Nonsense

---

*"She was up there ahead of me singing happily about how
wonderful the trails were as her horse moved gracefully
while I was coming behind her gritting my teeth as my
knees were skinned and banged up at every turn."*

**JEWEL GRIFFIN HAS** always been surrounded by family, friends, boarders, and neighbors who have been in her life many years, some for several decades.

But perhaps no one has spent more up close and personal time with Ms. Jewel during most of the past quarter century than Pamela Dwyer, a west Jacksonville transplant from Georgia.

It was 1998 when Dwyer decided to relocate from near Columbus to Jacksonville. She was just thirty-one-years-old and unmarried. Dwyer's first priority, even before finding a place to live, was locating a barn with pastures to board her horse, an Arabian.

"Before I moved, I drove down to scope out the horse boarding because that was more important than anything else," Dwyer recalled. In

Georgia, her horse had the run of 40 lush acres of pasture. She started her search near the beach where her boyfriend lived and "worked my way through every barn in the phone book."

She was shocked and disappointed to discover than none of the boarding barns had turnout or pasture. Her only option was a large field in neighboring MacClenny. "There was nowhere to ride, no one to ride with, no barn. But at least she would have grass," Dwyer said.

When she shared her frustration with some Jacksonville friends, one asked, "Have you tried Diamond D?" That turned out to be a life-altering question and brought Dwyer face to face with Jewel Griffin for the first time.

"When I arrived at Diamond D, I saw the huge pastures and the barns." She was directed to Ms. Jewel at the office "where I found this crisp, no-nonsense woman." Dwyer asked about boarding her Arabian. Jewel said board was $195 a month, feeding twice daily, and turn out all day. In addition to that, Diamond D's adjacent neighbor was state-owned Jennings Forest with miles of riding trails.

"But Ms. Jewel said there was only one stall left and if I wanted it, I had best give her a check right that moment, before it was gone." Dwyer says she was "a bit taken aback" by what she thought was a "bit of a brusque manner." She quickly wrote a check and began paying barn rental despite it being several months before her horse would arrive at Diamond D. "No way was I giving up my spot!"

Something about Dwyer let Ms. Jewel know pretty quickly that she not only had a new boarder, but someone who would be a riding buddy, traveling companion, and close friend. "I had been there just a couple of months trying to fit in and figure things out," when Jewel approached her at the barn. "She asked if I wanted to travel with her to a competitive trail ride." Dwyer, surprised, quickly said, "Yes."

Later she learned that Sonny Boy required Ms. Jewel to have a traveling companion when she went on rides. Dwyer also learned that her job traveling with Ms. Jewel was to provide conversation to keep her awake, and to make sure Ms. Jewel had a steady supply of Frito chips and cold Coke.

"I was a complete failure on the conversation at first," said Dwyer, so Ms. Jewel told her to play some of her music CDs. "We listened to Willie Nelson, and some hymns the rest of the drive."

After that first trip, the conversations came easier to Dwyer, "and sometimes we just sang the hymns together."

While traveling with Ms. Jewel was fun, Dwyer was not having that good a time with her own Arabian. "I was depressed about my lack of progress, and I just stopped going." Later, Dwyer went to Diamond D to pay her board. Ms. Jewel came out to meet her. "Where have you been girl? I was getting ready to call you to find out what was going on."

Surprised that Ms. Jewel had noticed her absence, Dwyer explained she was sad about her riding. Ms. Jewel offered to help. "I'm not an instructor and I can't tell you how to ride, but if you ride with me, I'll show you," Ms. Jewel said to Dwyer. It was the first of many times she heard that disclaimer of not being an instructor from Ms. Jewel over the next several years.

"This was the way Ms. Jewel has been with every person who took the time to go with her on rides, or who needed any help. She would always show people what she did and explain why she did it."

Eventually, in 2000 pupil Dwyer trained with Ms. Jewel and rode a full season of Competitive Trail with her. The season ended with the Florida Horsemen's Association two-day fifty-mile ride, followed by the three-day one-hundred-mile ride. "I wouldn't have finished if it had not been for Ms. Jewel." Dwyer said she was exhausted, her body ached, and she had blisters on both hands. "There were bloody sores on the inside of my knees where the stirrups had rubbed off my skin."

Dwyer said she "moaned and groaned and tried to bail out." Ms. Jewel was having none of it. "You're fine, your horse is doing great. Get on, let's go," she said, marching off to get her horse.

"How embarrassing to be half her age and feel like I was twice as old." The more Ms. Jewel rode, the fresher she got, Dwyer said.

"She was happy and proud of me and my horse when we'd get ribbons and win awards, even when we rode in the same category. Sometimes, I think she would forfeit her own success because she was looking out for the riders she brought with her."

On these long rides, Dwyer said Ms. Jewel was, "lighthearted and care-free, enjoying every moment with her horse." She would say, "Don't tell me anything about the barn while I'm gone."

Jewel Griffin was well-known in the competitive trail riding world, an intense competition that sometimes covers one-hundred-miles in two days. In fact, she was like a rock star because of her constant success. "It was like riding with a celebrity," Dwyer said. "Everyone wanted to say hello and see what she was up to and get her advice."

Sometimes, other riders would be disappointed to see her "because they knew she was always going to ride in the ribbons." Despite Ms. Jewel's persistent winning, "she never bragged about how good she was, or that she had a superior horse."

Ms. Jewel won because she spent hours in relentless practice before each competition. "She put in many hours on the trail and in the arena to prepare," Dwyer said. "She knew what kind of ride she wanted; she mapped out her ride in her head, and she knew the pace she would need to ride to complete the ride in a time that was good for her horse."

Some of the trails where she competed across the country were called, "Knee knockers that required your horse to bend skillfully to one side and immediately to the other as you moved between the trees." Dwyer recalled, "She was up there ahead of me singing happily about how wonderful the trails were as her horse moved gracefully while I was coming behind her gritting my teeth as my knees were skinned and banged up at every turn."

After riding the Competitive Trail competitions in 2000 with Ms. Jewel, Dwyer got married and moved to property a few miles from Diamond D. She and her husband became preoccupied with building their own horse barn and creating a grazing pasture. Dwyer still saw Ms. Jewel occasionally, but she missed riding with her. There was never enough time for working a full-time job, building and working a farm and riding. Then, Dwyer had a child, "and everything shifted."

When her maternity leave from teaching was over, she had it extended, then took a leave of absence. Ms. Jewel knew Dwyer didn't want to leave her little girl in nursery, but the young couple also needed income, Dwyer said. Ms. Jewel's life was also taking a turn as Sonny Boy built her the two-story log cabin on the lake that she always wanted, meaning they would be moving out of the century old cabin at Diamond D near the barn where the Griffins had lived since they moved to the ranch fifty years earlier.

"She just needed one thing: a reliable person to live at her original house who would listen to her instructions and follow them to the letter, while keeping up the relationships with people and horses that she'd created and nurtured for many years," Dwyer said.

One day in December 2004, the Griffins were moving out of the old log house while the Dwyer family was moving in. Pamela Dwyer worked for Ms. Jewel at the barn and lived with her family in that historic old house for seven years. Once her daughter, Haley, entered first grade, Dwyer returned to teaching.

"All of this would not have been possible if Mr. Sonny Boy had not agreed to take me on. We didn't have long conversations, but he would roll through the barn multiple times a day to survey the goings-on. He saw everything." Dwyer said in all the years she knew Sonny Boy, he never called her by her name. "I was always Georgia, and my daughter became Little Red because of the tint of her hair. My husband was Your Man. It was, "How's Your Man doing? How's Little Red today? How you doing, Georgia?"

Traveling with Ms. Jewel to look for a new horse, "was an education in itself." As they traveled the state, Ms. Jewel would meet the seller, walk out to the barn. "In just a few seconds Ms. Jewel would know (about the horse)." On one trip, Dwyer said she was "astounded" when Ms. Jewel quickly walked away from a great looking horse. "He had the itch," she said, meaning an itchy mane and tail. "I don't want to deal with that."

On another occasion, Dwyer said Ms. Jewel liked a horse, but turned him down because of a crook in his tail. "She would always tell us, 'You don't ride the head.'" That meant that if a horse is solid, don't turn it down because the head is not pretty.

After one of her buying trips, Ms. Jewel returned to Diamond D "with this scrawny, little bay Arabian gelding. She seemed a bit embarrassed about him, and said to several people, 'I only bought this horse because my husband told me I better come back with something this time.'"

The registered name of the horse was The Living Proof. He didn't have a barn name.

Ms. Jewel started riding the gelding in the round pen, and the next season, she decided to ride him in the Biltmore 100, a prestigious Competitive Endurance race in North Carolina. It rained relentlessly, filling up the stalls and leaking into the tent. A young boy nearby volunteered to help clean out the muddy stalls for Ms. Jewel. When he was finished, she asked the boy his name. "Chance," he said. "She decided right then to name that horse Chance," said Dwyer.

Unfortunately, it was Chance that almost cost Ms. Jewel her life the day she was out in Jennings Forest, training with her friend Laura Van Slyke and Dwyer. "On our ride, we passed the usual things like burntout stumps, mounds of odd-looking dirt, critters in the underbrush, and deer rustling in the glades. Her hew trail partner handed it with ease. It was his first trip in the forest, but he handled it like he'd been there a hundred times."

As the riders neared the end of the trail, Ms. Jewel "was rejoicing" how well Chance was doing. "The next moment, something radically changed. In one split-second, Chance went from a quiet, well-mannered trail horse to a terrified prey animal running for his life." Ms. Jewel screamed, "Whoa!" Dwyer tried to turn Chance to slow his dead run. It was too late. Jewel had lost her stirrups. "She smacked into a tree and silently fell to the ground."

Van Slyke got to Ms. Jewel first and quickly saw she was unconscious and bleeding underneath her helmet. Van Slyke stayed with the injured Jewel while Dwyer rode hurriedly for help. "From that day on, it was dark day after dark day waiting for news, praying Ms. Jewel would make it," said Dwyer.

During her recovery, Ms. Jewel, "was relentless in her determination," said Dwyer. "She was unwavering in her determination, seemingly unfazed by the hardships, the pain, and the long road to recovery."

Led by Sonny Boy, who wanted to shoot Chance, many members of the family were determined to get rid of the horse immediately. "She steadfastly refused to blame Chance for the accident and insisted she would ride him again one day." Months later, Ms. Jewel did ride Chance again to win many ribbons.

# Dreaming of Horses
# Turns into Nightmare

*"When I went in there the first time to see Momma,*
*I didn't even know it was Momma. God, her*
*head, I ain't never seen anything like it. If she*
*didn't have that helmet on, she'd be dead."*

SINCE HER VERY first memory, Jewel Griffin said the only thing she ever wanted to do was ride a horse.

As a child she dreamed about horses.

"Ever since I can remember, she wanted a horse. She didn't want a tricycle. She wanted a horse," said her sister Neni Jenkins, a year younger.

As a four-year-old, the family's next-door neighbor in Galveston was a night lookout guard who had a small horse living in his yard. Every night he hitched his horse to a buggy and drove it to work.

"He'd let me pet his horse. That's where I believe the horse got in-grained in me," Jewel recalled.

Little Jewel said she would catch Texas horny toads beneath her Galveston house. "I'd get me a matchbox and a string and hitch them toads to the boxes. That was my horse and buggy," she said.

When Jewel and her family lived in Winter Haven, Fl., she remembers, "I had access to a library. In the time I was there I read every horse book they had."

As a six-year-old, Jewel's family lived in Arkana, Arkansas for a brief time. The Stoddards owned two horses. The oldest was a gentle black mare. The other horse was younger. She became Jewel's very first horse. Her name was Topsy.

"I was petting her and playing with her all the time," said Jewel. One day, when her parents went to nearby Mountain Home for groceries, young Jewel said she led Topsy up to the side of the porch, and "I just got on her." The horse only had a halter and rope, no bridle or saddle.

"We just rode around in the yard. She did fine," Jewel said.

When her parents returned home, the excited child said, "Momma, I rode Topsy."

Her mother was not amused.

"Oh man. I got scolded. But I felt like I was in heaven."

In the nearly eight decades since that first ride on Topsy, Jewel Griffin has raced horses professionally, ridden in rodeos, and worked cows on the ranch. For the past twenty years she has competed nationally in long distance endurance races that are 25-100 miles long.

Jewel finally took her first riding lesson at age seventy-five after deciding she wanted to learn dressage.

"Some people are born to do things, and it just comes natural to them," said Jewel. "I think riding horses was just one thing I was born to do."

Anybody who rides horses regularly has a story to tell about their accidents, often resulting in broken bones.

Sometimes people die in horse mishaps.

Jewel Griffin has had her own share of injuries including a shattered collar bone, dislocated shoulder, back and neck surgery, and she has an artificial hip.

While seventy-four-year-old Jewel was training for a 100-mile competitive trail race, she had an accident that brought her face to face with death.

On this occasion, in February 2005, she was preparing to compete in the Biltmore 100, a prestigious and highly competitive endurance ride in North Carolina.

According to her riding companion and friend Pamela Dwyer, Jewel was following her normal routine to prepare. "She put in many hours on the trail and in the arena to prepare. That's why she won her races," said Dwyer.

Riding an Arabian gelding named Chance that she'd purchased on a recent buying trip, Jewel was in the forest at Diamond D. Riding with her were friends Laura Van Slyke and Dwyer.

Until this particular day, Jewel had only ridden Chance in the round pen, near the barn, and around the block. This was her first trip on Chance into Jennings Forest.

"We'd already ridden ten miles," said Jewel. He was doing really good, she said. "He was riding like an old broke horse."

"Chance handled it like he'd been there a hundred times," said Dwyer.

Toward the end of the ride, Jewel said she became negligent. "I was sitting up there like I was riding a quarter horse," she said, riding with her reins out. "We were relaxing and talking on the way home."

Without warning, Chance bolted, causing Jewel to lose both stirrups. "I didn't have him collected up in my hands."

"Whoa!" screamed Jewel.

Dwyer tried to turn the terrified Chance to slow his flight.

It was too late.

"He ran out through the woods," recalled Jewel.

"That's the last thing I remember."

"She smacked into a tree and silently fell to the ground," said Dwyer.

The impact of hitting the tree busted Jewel's helmet, "and laid my eye out on my face," she said.

Van Slyke reached Jewel first. She saw that she was unconscious and bleeding beneath her helmet.

Van Slyke remained with Jewel while Dwyer raced for help.

Dwyer found Jewel's daughter, Cathy, who phoned Sonny Boy. He quickly raced his truck into the forest where Jewel lay near death on the ground.

"He knew where I come off the horse," said Jewel.

Sonny Boy also knew an ambulance would not be able to reach her through the thick woods.

"I'm putting her in the truck," Sonny Boy told Van Slyke.

An ambulance met Sonny Boy's truck at the at the hard road by the barn.

"They tried to get a Life Flight helicopter for me, but it was in Houston," said Jewel.

Jewel said doctors told her family, "If I lived, I wasn't going to be nothing but a vegetable."

"That was the scariest day of my life," said daughter Dr. Tammy Jordan. "I was working in my yard, and somebody came running up and said they were trying to get her out of the forest."

Fifty-year-old Griffin son Michael was at a horse show in the Jacksonville Equestrian Center on Normandy Blvd., a short distance from Diamond D. His sister, Tammy, called him. "We were all scared to death. We didn't know how bad it was," said Michael.

The ambulance raced the dying legendary equestrian to University Hospital. Inside with his mother was Michael. Just behind the ambulance was Sonny Boy's truck. Tammy was driving.

During the rushed drive to the hospital, Tammy said Michael kept phoning the truck. "You got to get daddy here. She's not going to make it," he said frantically. "It was very scary," said Tammy.

When the family reached the hospital, "It really got scary. They talked about pulling the plug on her."

The family phoned a priest.

When Jewel's sister, Neni Jenkins, reached the hospital, "They wouldn't let me in to see her," she said.

As the priest came down the hospital hall and started to pass by Neni, "I told him who I was and that they wouldn't let anybody else in but the clergy."

The priest handed Neni a Bible. "You're my Bible carrier," he said.

"Then he took me right in to see my sister. That was a wonderful blessing, that I was able to speak to her even though she couldn't hear me."

Twenty-five-year-old granddaughter Jodi Coxwell was in Perry, Georgia at a horse cutting competition when she learned of the accident. "They told me they didn't know if she was going to make it. I just drove faster than ever on I-75 coming back from Perry. It took the wind out of us."

"When I went in there the first time to see Momma," said daughter Cathy, "I didn't even know it was Momma. God, her head, I ain't never seen anything like it. If she didn't have that helmet on, she'd be dead."

By all accounts, her mother's head was swollen to the size of a pumpkin. Jewel was beyond recognition, even to members of her family.

Tammy, a veterinarian, became the family liaison with the hospital medical staff. "She kind of run everything," said Michael. "I never left the hospital," said Tammy.

The Griffins also had a friend who was a head nurse at the hospital "and he really looked after Momma."

"I felt blessed that my aunt (Tammy Jordan) was a vet and could help us understand the medical terminologies," said Jodi Coxwell.

Jewel lay in the hospital unconscious for 13 days. Family members and close friends stayed by her side and in constant prayer.

Eighty-year-old Rodney Butler has been a constant presence at Diamond D since 1976. "I was in shock," he said. "Diamond D Ranch is Jewel Griffin."

"From that day on, it was dark day after dark day waiting for news, praying Ms. Jewel would make it," said Dwyer.

"It was like a pallor came over this place. Everyone was a little on edge. There was a lot of praying," longtime Diamond D boarder Margaret Durrett said,

"I was at the Ford place getting my truck and my daughter called," said Jewel's oldest friend, Jane Wiggins. "I just broke down and cried."

"If she had died, Uncle Sonny Boy would have died right there with her," said nephew Terry Freeman. "I went up there and he was crying like a baby."

After fighting for her life for almost two weeks, Jewel woke up.

Tiffany and her Aunt Neni were visiting Jewel when she came out of her coma. "I held her hand and she kept trying to say something. She couldn't write anything down." Tiffany said, "'Granny, slow down.' I finally figured out what she was trying to say."

"Barn," Jewel whispered.

"She was worried about that barn while she was in the hospital."

Tiffany said, "I got it. The barn is taken care of." Tiffany, daughter of Tammy and Jerry Jordan, was sixteen. She worked at the barn to help her Granny.

"On the fourteenth day, they sent me home," she said.

Jewel's sister Neni temporarily moved from her home in Gainesville to help care for her. "They had to bind her mouth," said Neni, who remained with Jewel for four weeks. "I was hand-feeding her until she was able to do something for herself."

Other family members also helped around the clock.

A steel plate was inserted into Jewel's face, and she was stitched severely.

On the day Neni took her back to the hospital to have the stiches removed, while sitting in the waiting room, Jewel said, "People were in there fighting." The security guard removed Jewel and Neni.

Hospital personnel placed Jewel onto a gurney and moved her upstairs.

After the stitches were removed, she saw the doctor who had performed the surgery on her head. "I walked in his office, and he said, 'Oh my gosh. Lady, you are a miracle. I didn't think I would ever see you walk again.'"

Jewel replied, "It's that Man upstairs. He's the only one who knew it wasn't my time."

Sonny Boy was lost without Jewel. She wasn't just his business partner. She was his caretaker, fixing his meals, making sure he stayed on a proper diet, and giving Sonny Boy his insulin shots.

As normal, when there is a crisis or emergency, the entire Griffin family rallies. During Jewel's recovery, everyone made sure Sonny Boy was cared for.

"We just all took care of him," said granddaughter Tiffany. "We made sure he had food on the table. He was sad, but he tried to act like everything was going to be all right."

Sonny Boy wanted to shoot Chance after the accident, but family members convinced him to spare the horse's life. "Everybody convinced him that shooting a horse ain't going to help nothing," said Jewel.

"The next morning, Big Daddy was going to kill the horse," recalled Tiffany.

"Big Daddy, stop! You're not going to shoot it. That's not something she would want," Tiffany told her grandfather.

The family wanted Chance moved off the ranch. Jewel wouldn't have it. She was determined to ride Chance again and return to endurance competitions.

Sonny Boy told Cathy to start riding Chance. "My daddy said to make that horse run away from me, then pull him down and make him stop," she said.

Cathy placed sticks, plastic bags, and jugs filled with rocks all over the horse. "I put a thing around his butt. I tried to make that horse run away but I couldn't get him any faster than a canter. But I did put a stop on him."

Once she regained consciousness, nobody doubted that her faith and fighting spirit would carry Jewel to recovery.

"She was relentless in her determination," said Dwyer. "She did the exercises her doctors told her to do and refrained from doing what she was told not to do. Ms. Jewel was unwavering in her determination, seemingly unfazed by the hardships, the pain and the long road to recovery."

"She gets knocked down and she pops back up. She has the desire to pop back up and go at it again," said her sister, Neni.

"I didn't worry because I just knew she was going to be okay. That's her," said granddaughter Amy. "You can't keep her down."

"Man, she's a survivor. She's been through a lot of stuff," said her oldest friend, Jane Wiggins. "She's like a warrior."

In June, just three months after the accident, Jewel had not only defied death, but she was also back riding Chance.

"It felt wonderful. I rode all through the woods. I wasn't ready to give up riding."

She started training again for endurance. Within time, Jewel and Chance qualified for the Arabian National Championship ride in Leatherwood, NC.

In her comeback race, she missed winning the gold by only half a point, coming in second and gaining the title of National Reserve Champion.

Afterwards, she said, "I probably won ten 100-mile rides with him."

Eight years after her near-tragic wreck on Chance, Jewel began training again for endurance competitions on a different horse. Chance had passed away from colic.

Jewel was eighty-two.

Her training ended abruptly when her new horse threw her into a creek. She shattered her collar bone and dislocated her shoulder.

Now eighty-four, Jewel is training again, this time for shorter 25-mile competitions.

For one of her granddaughters, K'leigh Griffin Combs, Jewel's fight through life- threatening injuries became an inspiration she modeled when K'Leigh faced her own dire health issues.

"I had an accident when I was pregnant with my son," she said. "I was 28 weeks pregnant when I got backed over by a horse trailer." She broke her hip, sacrum and had five fractures in her back.

The evening the accident happened, doctors told K'Leigh they were going to perform an emergency C section. K'Leigh, who was in terrible pain, said, "No, you're not."

Doctors explained that if something was wrong with her organs, a C section will let them remove the baby.

She thought about the fight and courage shown by her grandmother following her horse accident. "I remembered how tough she was. She always knew she'd get through it. There was no doubt in her mind."

Doctors stressed they needed to perform the surgery. K'Leigh asked if her body could heal itself without surgery. It's possible, the doctors said, but not likely. "They told me I was broke in half," said K'Leigh. She said her final answer was, "No. I have prayed about it, and God is going to take care of this."

K'Leigh just wanted to know if her baby was okay.

She was on her back and couldn't walk for three months, but she managed to carry the baby to thirty-seven weeks before delivering by C section.

Just like her Gran Jewel, K'Leigh said, "I remember thinking the whole time that I've got to be tough like her, toughen up. And I did."

She and her husband, Dusty, named the baby boy Griffin to carry on the family name of Sonny Boy, which pleased the old cowboy very much. He joked the child with that name will have a lot to live up to.

Later, K'Leigh and Dusty had a little girl they named Dal'Leigh Louise.

# Growing Up Grandchildren of Diamond D Ranch

---

*"I really think the country background is unique to our family. There were so many different things to do. We went from riding to hunting to fishing to cattle and boarding and rental stables."*

GROWING UP AS a child at Diamond D Ranch was a mystical experience for Jodi Griffin Coxwell, her sisters Amy Griffin and K'Leigh Griffin Combs, and cousins Marty and Tony Higdon, Casey Melton Garner, Travis Jordan, and his sister Tiffany Jordan Williamson.

The days were full of demanding work and hours upon hours in the saddle, racing through the woods, working cows alongside their dads and grandfather, and hunting deer, turkey and quail in the forests and fields at the ranch.

"I really think the country background is unique to our family," said Amy.

"As a kid, I was able to throw my legs across a horse when I was four-years-old. I got a lot of my passion for riding horses from my Granny," said Jodi, the oldest of Jewel and Sonny Boy Griffin's five granddaughters.

"When I was about five, I followed her through the woods." In elementary school, before she caught the bus, Jodi rode with her grandmother. "I learned it was hard to get up, ride and be back, and have your horse put up before school."

Her rides with Jewel were serious. "I wanted to talk a little more. She wanted to ride at a certain pace, and it was hard to keep up with Granny when I was little. I can keep up with her now."

"We had the best backyard in the world. I could ride from here to Orange Park, or here to Clay Hill, and never see a paved road," she said.

"We picked Mayhaw and made Mayhaw jelly. Big Daddy would take me to pick a bucket full of blackberries and we'd make blackberry jelly and cobblers."

Diamond D was just as enriching and fun for the Griffin family boys. "We went fishing every day, snake hunting every day," said grandson Tony. "I was always out on the woods trapping hogs or killing deer, just riding looking for fence that was down."

Tony's older brother Marty loved hunting with his grandfather. He learned quickly when chores were finished each day, there were lots of fun things to do. "We helped feed up and get the horses out in the morning. We helped Gran Jewel saddle the horses and get them ready to go out," he said. "We guided a few trail rides."

Travis Jordan was the third grandson of the Griffins. Unfortunately, Travis passed away at age 36 from complications as a result of a terrible automobile accident ten years earlier. The accident left him paralyzed from the waist down and the once active young man spent his last years in a wheelchair.

"Travis was just as onery as Big Daddy," said his sister Tiffany.

"Once, when we were about 12, Travis got this bright idea to take an old tractor tire and put a rope on it, tie it up to the back of a 4-wheeler, and drag all of us around the barn yard," she said. "It was like a tube behind a boat in the river."

After all of the kids, including Travis, had their turn, they decided to go to their grandparents' house. "We were as black as the Ace of Spades from head to toe. It's a wonder we didn't get killed," recalled Tiffany.

They never made it inside the house. Their granny made sure of that. "Granny caught us on the porch. We all got in trouble and had to be hosed off in the barnyard."

Like all of the Griffin grandchildren, Travis did his share of chores, opened gates for Sonny Boy and hunted with his Big Daddy at the Yellow Water Hunt Club.

As part of his rehabilitation and recreation, Sonny Boy taught Travis how to moonshine. "At least every other day, Big Daddy would ride by and coach Travis on how to maintain and condition the moonshine still," said Tiffany. "He had an agreement with Trav that every batch he cooked, Big Daddy would get a gallon out of it for taste testing."

Travis passed away ten months after Sonny Boy's death. He is buried next to his grandfather in Deese Cemetery.

While he wasn't officially a grandchild, Donnie Wynn was treated like one because he was the son of Sonny Boy's best friend Donald Wynn.

Donnie spent most of his youth and has lived at Diamond D his adult life. "I remember feeding the hogs and going to get the swill," he said.

He recalls one occasion when he and Robbie Freeman worked all day as young teenagers, then spent the night in Jewel's office in the barn. "I had an old guitar, and we'd write some songs," said Wynn. "There used to be signs all over those woods that said, 'Cows and Hogs are protected by A.D. Griffin and son.' One night, me and Robbie wrote a song and that was basically the brunt of it."

Looking back, Wynn said, "Our parents probably put us out there to keep us out of trouble."

"There were so many different things to do," said Amy. "We went from riding to hunting to fishing to cattle and boarding and rental stables. We had hayrides on the weekends with Granny. If we weren't showing horses, we were working with the ranch horses and doing pony rides. I ran the stables when I was old enough."

"Big Daddy let me be a boy," said Jodi, who started hunting with her father as a three-year-old. She first hunted with her grandfather when she was five. "I remember having to grab his dogs and they were as big as I was. I was thinking, these things need a bath."

Jodi shot her first deer when she was in the sixth grade. "I shot it with a 4-10 slug. Everybody was all excited, but I run away because I knew I was fixing to get bloodied." Blooding a hunter after the first deer kill is a ritual with roots centuries ago. Usually, a parent or member of the hunt camp applies blood from the deer to the hunter's face.

The boys on the hunt chased after her. "My daddy yelled, 'You'd better come back here.' They bloodied me good." Her father and grandfather also "got in on it."

"Big Daddy taught me everything about hunting. I learned to turkey call from Big Daddy, and I can turkey call with my mouth," Jodi said.

Jodi knew as a youngster that she was lucky. "I knew it wasn't what every child did because by the time I got on the bus, I would pass other houses and they weren't like mine. I knew my childhood was special."

The Griffin granddaughters became accomplished riders at young ages, starting about as soon as they shed their diapers. It wasn't just relaxed riding for fun in the woods. Competitions drove their passions and fueled their dreams.

All three of Michael and Galynna's daughters have shown pleasure horses in 4-H at district and state levels.

Jodi Griffin Coxwell has competed in showing cutting horses, once finishing sixth in the world at the National Cutting Horse Association competition. She won both Georgia and Alabama cutting competitions and won reserve in Florida. Jodi was Miss Jacksonville Rodeo Queen.

She continues to compete running barrels while raising and training horses. She has a herd of cattle at her husband David and Jodi's C3 Ranch.

Like her own grandmother, Jewel, she has cemented her reputation as an outstanding equestrian.

Jodi's daughters Madison and Graci (great granddaughters of Jewel and Sonny Boy) have won several rodeo titles at the district, state and national level. They compete in barrels, poles, goat tying and breaking roping.

Jodi and David's son, J.D., is not a competing equestrian. Instead, he plays football and hunts squirrels that he brings to his Granny to cook. "Nobody can cook squirrel like Granny Jewel," said J.D.

Middle sister Amy Griffin was an accomplished equestrian in her own right as a youngster, winning pony classes and being named Miss Jacksonville Rodeo Queen like her sister Jodi. She was chosen Miss Baldwin High School and was Salutatorian of her class at Baldwin High School

The youngest of the three sisters, K'Leigh said, "I've shown western pleasure, rode cutting horses, and I've rodeoed." Her list of competitions also includes barrels, poles, team roping, and goat tying.

In 2006, K'Leigh was Florida High School Rodeo Queen. "Big Daddy had the biggest smile on his face when I brought him that crown. He was tickled to death." She also won Miss Congeniality at the NHSR finals.

K'Leigh also shared a love of turkey hunting with her Big Daddy. "When I was 18, I killed two turkeys with one shot."

"Big Daddy always would tell me if I just sit there and call, that turkey will come around. You just have to have patience," an irony from Sonny Boy that was amusing to K'Leigh. "You have patience?" she thought but didn't say.

Like sister Jodi, K'Leigh can also call a turkey with her mouth.

Amy recalls a day as a six-year-old when her Big Daddy, father, and sister Jodi were going hunting together. Her mother, Galynna, had made a huge lunch for everyone. "It looked like something out of a magazine you're about to eat. We were looking forward to it."

As they were leaving, her dad and Jodi got in Michael's truck. "Dad said for me to get in the truck with Big Daddy."

Sonny Boy's hounds were running. "You get out there and catch that dog," Sonny Boy told her. "So, I get out there." Catching running dogs can be tough for anyone, especially a six-year-old girl. "When I came out of the woods, I was soaking wet and dirty from head to toe."

All she wanted, she said, was a shower and something to eat. Thinking about the scrumptious lunch her mother had made, Amy told Sonny Boy, "All right Big Daddy, I'm hungry." Sonny Boy said, okay, and told her he had some food.

"He hands me some sardines and crackers. They're eating all that good food and I'm stuck eating sardines and catching dogs."

When Tiffany Jordan Williamson was growing up at Diamond D, her mother was attending vet school in Gainesville, and her dad worked nights. "So, I spent a lot of time out here with my Granny and Big Daddy."

After school each day, the bus would let her off at the end of Solomon Road near the boarding barn. "I stayed with Granny until my mom got home from school each day," she said.

As a homeschooled 15-year-old, Tiffany told her grandmother she was bored. Jewel asked if she wanted to start feeding the horses. "Every morning at 7 a.m., I'd be down there feeding and letting them out. Then, I'd come back about 2:30, let them in and feed them again."

Tiffany said that's when she learned about having responsibility.

Sometimes, she worked with her Big Daddy, riding in his truck. Sonny Boy had a well-earned reputation for always having someone with him to open the many gates on the ranch.

Tiffany remembers thinking the only reason Sonny Boy wanted her with him was to open gates. "Get that gate, granddaughter," he would say, prompting Tiffany to once tell her parents and grandmother, "I don't think Big Daddy knows my name. He just says 'granddaughter' all the time."

Jodi also remembers opening lots of gates. "You didn't walk. You ran. And you knew if you were supposed to shut that gate or leave it open. You always left the gate the way you found it, or you were in trouble."

Like the other Griffin granddaughters, Tiffany became an exceptional rider. When she outgrew her pony, Jewel gave Tiffany her first horse. "It was an old Arabian and the ugliest thing in the world. His name was Hodge."

Tiffany competed in western pleasure and ran barrels. Once she decided to ride English in a 4H show, using Jewel's saddle. "I won the show. I said, 'I'm going to try this.'"

For a while, Tiffany ran barrels with her mother, Dr. Jordan, and she continued to run barrels until her son, Kaiden, turned five and began playing T-ball. "You can't go to both," she said.

Tiffany shot her first deer as an eleven-year-old. Hunting with Big Daddy, she said, "was exciting. Sometimes we'd be in the truck, and he would yell, 'Hang on.' We'd probably be going sixty miles an hour down a dirt road."

K'Leigh recalls as a six-year-old riding with her parents, Granny Jewel, and Big Daddy in the Jennings State Forest together. Sonny Boy was on his four-wheeler, and the others rode horses.

"My dad noticed there was a cow that had a big bag, and he knew she had a calf somewhere," said K'Leigh. Her grandfather said a coyote probably got it. They should just ride on.

"After a few minutes, I heard a calf bellow off in the distance," said

K'Leigh. Her Big Daddy didn't believe her. Her dad, Michael, told K'Leigh to ride in the direction she heard the bellow. Her mother and Granny Jewel stayed behind to hold the cows while K'Leigh, her dad, and Big Daddy rode off to try and find the calf.

"I was on my pony, and I rode over to a pump shed and there was the calf." The calf was weak, and the men said it had probably been trapped in the shed for a couple of days.

"My daddy took the calf and threw him across my saddle with me."

Later, when Sonny Boy sold the calves, "He made sure I got the money for that calf."

Casey Melton Garner was first on a horse with her mother, trainer Cathy, when she was four months old. "At one, Casey rode by herself," said her mom.

At three, she showed a horse. "Casey was beating the stew out of all these kids out here in western pleasure and showmanship when she was three-years-old," said her mother.

But as Casey grew older, she wanted to put Diamond D in her rear-view mirror. "I ran from these woods. I was born and raised in the country, and I wanted to get out." It was a decision she seems to regret, at least a little.

"When I look back, I wish my kids could have lived the life I had out here. I remember at five running around the barn yard catching biddies without a parent standing over us. I can imagine what my momma's life was like because of how I grew up."

# Do it First, Do it Well ... or Else

———❦———

*"We got one of the worst ass whippings I ever got in my entire life when we wanted to go to the creek and swim one day. We just stuck the watering hose in the hole just enough to get some water on the wood where it looked like you'd watered them horses."*

MARTY HIGDON, THE Griffin's first-born grandchild, learned the painful way that when you had chores to do at Diamond D Ranch, you better do them first, and do them well. No shortcuts, no faking it.

A primary ranch job for Marty and the other kids at Diamond D was to water all of the stalled horses kept in the big barns. "They had little holes drilled in the stalls where you stuck the hose through," said Higdon. "You stand there and wait until you hear the water running out of the bucket, then you go to the next stall."

The lure of all the distractions from ranch work were so strong it just naturally pulled the kids away from their chores before they were finished. After all, fishing, swimming, riding horses, and hunting were a lot more fun than work.

"We got one of the worst ass whippings I ever got in my entire life when we wanted to go to the creek and swim one day," recalled Higdon. To speed up the watering process, "We just stuck the watering hose in the hole just enough to get some water on the wood where it looked like you'd watered them horses."

Marty's younger brother, Tony, was supposed to help water the horses that day. He remembers that whipping well. "Granny Jewel straightened us out. She could get on that tail, now," said Tony.

It was a trick tried more than once, despite Jewel almost always noticing.

"Somehow, they got the idea if they wet the front of the stall, I'd think they watered the horses," said Jewel. "I'm a little smarter than they were."

Jewel always checked to see if there was water in the buckets. If the buckets were empty, "They got their butts busted and they couldn't have tea for supper. If the horses don't get no water, you don't get no tea."

"We made like it was done, and we told Gran Jewel it was done. Then we hauled on down to the creek."

Shortly, Jewel was also at the creek. "She come with a set of old reins and whipped our asses all the way back to the barn. We finished watering them horses."

Marty grew up in nearby Maxville, a short distance through the woods from Diamond D. Like most of the Griffin grandchildren, Marty and his younger brother Tony were drawn to Diamond D by their grandparents and the magnetism of all there was for kids to do at the ranch.

"We lived across the creek. One weekend I'd be hunting with my daddy over there, and the next weekend I'd be hunting with my grandpa," said Marty. Before leaving for Diamond D, Marty said he would, "get a lecture from my daddy. 'Don't go over there with your grandpa and be killing them damn does and give us Higdons a bad name.'"

When he would leave Big Daddy to hunt with his father, Marty said Sonny Boy would warn, "Don't you go over there and be killing them damn does with those Higdons and be giving us a bad name over here."

Higdon remembers when he was ten years old that he went hunting one day with Sonny Boy at the Cecil Field Rod and Gun Club, which butted up to the back of Diamond D. "He always had a good pack of deer hounds," he said.

"He took a couple of dogs and went walking in the woods." While he was away from the truck, Aaron Coleman called on the CB. Since Sonny Boy wasn't there, young Marty responded.

"Big Daddy's out here in the woods," he told Coleman.

"He got any dogs? We just seen a buck."

"Uncle Aaron, there's some dogs in here, but these must not be good ones because he didn't take them with him," Marty answered.

Sonny Boy was too far from the truck to hear any of the CB conversation.

When he got back, he heard Coleman and other hunters joking with Marty about what he had said. "I was a little bitty fellow, and I didn't know you only take a couple of dogs at a time."

Coleman wasn't about to pass up a chance to poke at his friend, Sonny Boy. "Hell, I thought everything he had was good hounds."

When Higdon was a kid, Diamond D was home to several large peacocks. The male peacock has large, beautiful tail feathers. "They're the prettiest feathers you ever seen," said Marty.

After mating season each year, the male peacocks lose their feathers in a process called molting.

Marty, his brother Tony, cousin Jason Freeman, and Shane Coleman decided to turn those peacock feathers into a profit-making business.

"When the city folks come out there and rent the horses, they liked to buy them peacock feathers," he said. "All them women at the barn would give us $1 for a tail feather," said Tony.

So, after mating season each year, the boys would collect the lose feathers and sell them.

"We had us a monopoly on peacock feathers," he said.

"It was the time of the year when they weren't shedding no feathers, and this couple comes out here that had bought some feathers before."

The woman asked Marty if she could get some more peacock feathers.

"How many do you want?"

"Eight or ten," she said.

While Jewel was giving her standard instructions to the two riders, the boys, "devised us a plan."

They found a bucket. "We was going to get us peacock feathers."

The boys cornered a male peacock in the aisle between the stalls in one of the barns. "We caught that joker and plucked that fella of every bright feather he had," recalled Marty. "We caught that peacock by the tail and snatched them all out," said Tony.

After the couple returned from their ride, Jewel saw them walking to their car carrying the freshly picked tail feathers.

Then she saw the boys.

"She called me over and asked, 'Where did y'all get all them feathers?'"

"Granny, we chased one of them peacocks down over there in the barn and plucked his feathers out."

"You did what?"

"We chased a peacock down in the barn and plucked his feathers out. They was wanting some more feathers and we didn't have none." The peacock's tail feathers had just grown back, meaning it would be another year before they would return.

Punishment was swift and sure.

Every Friday night, Jewel and Sonny Boy held hayrides into the woods where they cooked hotdogs and marshmallows over a fire. The day before each outing, Marty and the other kids would cut about fifty palmetto limbs to turn into hotdog sticks.

"Granny cut her one of them palmetto stakes and lined us on the hitching post. She whupped our tails for plucking that old peacock. We never messed with a peacock no more."

On another occasion, Marty, Tony, and Shane were instructed by Sonny Boy to plant pine seedlings on a piece of land that had been clear-cut of trees. The boys were given eight sacks of baby pines, along with a digging instrument that was, "two little steel handles with a wedge on the bottom. You push the handle back and forth and make a little hole," said Marty. "You'd drop a little pine tree down in it, just stomp on both sides of it, and straighten the little pine tree up in the hole."

Sonny Boy dropped off the boys, tools, and pine seedlings to start planting. "He'd take you in there and go off somewhere to work. He left them with nothing to eat or drink. "It was hot in the summer."

Usually, when Sonny Boy returned, he would bring the boys a soft drink and a sandwich.

"We had been planting them pine trees and planting them pine trees. We thought we'd planted enough, so we started putting two or three pine trees in each hole. It was about 2 o'clock or so and he ain't brought us no sandwich. We was right above the three bridges, so we run down to the creek to get some water out of the creek," Marty said.

That's when Sonny Boy drove up.

"Here he comes," recalled Marty. "He was raising cane that we'd took a break and we wasn't supposed to take a break until he come back. That was about the only time he whupped me."

For years, every time Marty and Sonny Boy would return to the area where the pines were planted, Sonny Boy would say, "Look at the crooked pine trees y'all planted out here, grandson."

# SAN MARCO TO DIAMOND
# D TO THE COURTHOUSE

~~~

*"He was just showing himself, being an ass, and still cussing. Sonny Boy walked up to him, hit him one time in the jaw, knocked him on the ground."*

*Laying where he'd landed, the guy looked up at Sonny Boy and asked, "You do that to all your customers'"*

*"No," said Sonny Boy. "Just the ones that cuss at my wife and run my horses."*

YOUNG LANCE DAY grew up in Jacksonville's southside community of San Marco. With its white-collar working families and trendy neighborhoods, San Marco was twenty-five miles away and a world apart from the blue-collar west Jacksonville of wide-open spaces and Diamond D Ranch.

Lance was an only child who says his parents were his best friends. His dad was a claims supervisor at Liberty Mutual and his mom was a community volunteer.

By all accounts, his parents thought 11-year-old Lance was living a much too sheltered life. A colleague of Mr. Day's at Liberty Mutual often took her children out to Diamond D to ride the rental horses.

One day, while the Griffins were away buying horses, "She said she was house sitting at the ranch for a couple of weeks. She suggested my parents bring me out," Lance recalls.

Sonny Boy and Jewel had just arrived home from their horse-buying trip the day Lance and his parents drove to Diamond D. "I immediately took to the place and just loved it," said Lance. He had ridden horses in a ring, but nothing like this.

Over time, the Days saw how happy Lance was at Diamond D. His dad decided to drive Lance to the ranch every weekend. It was fifty miles round trip from San Marco. Each day Mr. Day would take Lance out in the morning and return to pick him up later in the day.

"My dad was driving one hundred miles a day just to let me go out to Diamond D. It became a weekend thing," said Lance.

Like so many of the children who counted Diamond D as a home away from home, Lance eventually became acclimated to ranch life. He and the Griffin's son, Michael, became good friends. "One day, Ms. Jewel told my parents, 'Why don't you just let him stay out here?' I became kind of like their extra kid on the weekend."

Before they turned him over to the Griffins, Lance's parents made something very clear. "Treat him like your own. If he gets out of line, treat him like your own." That meant the Griffins enforced discipline, and chores came before play. "We would have our system. We'd clean out the stalls, feed the horses, water them, get them out in the pasture. Then after we did those things, we'd help saddle up the rental horses. Once Ms. Jewel got the rentals going in the morning, it gave us some free time."

"I'm a loving person, but I'm also kind of a strict person," says Ms. Jewel. "If you've got a job to do, you've got that job to do. They would come out here and I would say, 'When the work gets done y'all can go play.'"

Free time for the kids was always hard-earned and well-spent. "We'd go out exploring all day. Sonny Boy had a lease from Gilman (Paper Co.), so he had access to about 18,000 acres. It was just huge and went all the way over to the air base. We'd ride all through the woods exploring."

"We were like brothers," said Michael. "Lance could ride a horse really good. We'd get on a horse and leave out of here, pack us a lunch. We'd come home at dusk. If we came home after dark, we got in trouble."

Michael recalled a time with Lance when the movie "Mary Poppins" was popular. "We got us some umbrellas and decided to jump out of a tree. We went up in the tree about 12 or 14 feet and Lance coached me to go first. The umbrella held me for a minute, then that son of a gun broke loose. When I fell and hit the ground, Lance decided not to jump with his umbrella."

Michael's granddaddy, Dewey Griffin, had a dilapidated, old Willis Jeep. "It had no brakes, and the floorboard was rotted out. You could see the ground. We would ride the woods in that jeep for hours, until we ran out of gas. The only way to stop was just slow it down, keep gearing down, then you would ease into a ditch or a tree."

"It (the Jeep) was like a tank," said Michael. "We found third gear and I found a tree at the same time and throwed Lance up on the hood. Wonder it didn't kill him."

Today, Judge Day admits that at first, he was not a skilled rider like the Griffin children, or some of the other kids who hung out at the ranch. He rode the Griffin's horses because he didn't have one of his own.

Before investing in a horse, his parents wanted to make sure "this wasn't just a phase I was going through."

After about two years, one of Sonny Boy's friends, Aaron Coleman, decided to sell his horse, Poco. Ms. Jewel suggested to Lance's parents that Poco would be a good horse for Lance. "They were not using him, and he'd just been left out in the pasture," said Lance. The Days purchased Poco for $300. "We started boarding him at Diamond D, and to keep my costs down, my job was to help clean out the stalls and help keep the horses watered for everybody else."

He loved the barn work. "But if you told me to mow my lawn, I couldn't stand it."

Because Poco had been left in the pasture and not ridden, he was "big, fat, and overweight." Poco was also onery. "He was going to do things his way. And he had a disposition that was just not nice. I became afraid of him, but I didn't want to tell my parents because I was afraid they'd sell him."

The ever-observant Ms. Jewel quickly recognized what was happening. "One day she snatched me up at the corral said very plainly, 'You're letting that horse be your boss. If you aren't going to take control of that horse, show that horse you're the person in control, I'm going to tell your parents to sell him.'"

Then, Ms. Jewel took over. "I'm going to show you your horse can be trained immediately to do the things you want to do. So, get off him." Ms. Jewel got on the horse, and "within two minutes he had a complete change in disposition. She said, 'Now this is the way your horse will respond if he knows you're in control and you're the boss.'" Ms. Jewel dismounted. "Now, get back on."

During those weekends and summers of his youth, the city boy from

San Marco kept pace with the Griffin kids and the other country children at Diamond D. "It was things kids dream of doing." There were campfires and night rides, an annual cattle drive to check the new-born calves and mark them. "That taught you restraint and maturity. I didn't realize at the time these were all little tests."

Poco was a great riding companion for young Lance, but one day it all sadly came to an end. "Mr. Griffin called my dad, and I knew something was wrong." Lance and his dad drove out to Diamond D. When they arrived, the veterinarian was already there. "It was one of the first times I saw Ms. Jewel visibly upset." She told us Poco had tested positive for Coggins." Coggins is a worldwide infectious disease spread when a horse fly bites an infected horse and then bites a healthy horse.

"In those days, they didn't understand Coggins, so they were destroying horses all over the country. My dad told the vet, 'We're not going to destroy this horse.'" At first, Poco was isolated in a corral on the ranch until a plan was made to move him.

Mr. Day had a friend who owned a Chevrolet dealership in Georgia. He had several children and had been looking for a horse he could trust around his kids. The Days gifted Poco to the family. "It was amazing. Poco was one of those horses who knew a child. A child could pull his tail and he wouldn't do anything. A child could walk underneath him."

For years, Lance said Poco "lived a great life. It was a sad way ending in that way for me, but it was a good ending for him."

Lance never bought another horse, but he continued to ride regularly at Diamond D.

His next equine buddy was Ms. Jewel's show horse, Murphy Sick 'Em. "Murphy was one of those kinds of horses that if you rode him, you did everything you were supposed to do. If you didn't, he'd throw you off."

When Ms. Jewel started letting Lance ride Murphy, "it was a source of pride for me because I knew if you were riding that horse, it was because you were doing everything you were supposed to do and doing it the right way. I would walk around saying, 'I'm riding Murphy Sic 'Em.' That was a point of pride for me."

Lance Day was elected Circuit Court Judge for Florida's 4th Circuit in 1996, and re-elected in 2002, 2008, 2014, and 2020. He always has had the support of the Griffins. "There was not a politician I can recall that didn't come out to Diamond D and meet with Sonny Boy and Jewel, hoping to get their support because that would give them a big chunk of the westside."

As a judge, Day says he applies many of the practical life lessons in his court that he learned as a young person at Diamond D. "You can't cut corners when you have animals like that. You can't cut corners when you're a judge. You have to read up on the law. You've got to study and stay up on things. When you're grooming a horse, you might want to get out and ride, and so you might not brush him down thorough. You throw the saddle blanket on him, then throw on the saddle, but he's still got dirt under there, and all of a sudden, you've got a saddle sore. Those are lessons you carry on. Everything has to be done properly."

Day says, "Growing up at Diamond D molded me. I noticed that I would go to school in town, and frankly, I felt more mature than a lot of the people around me because of what I was doing out at Diamond D."

Some of the lessons Day learned came the hard way, like reasoning. "A lot of things sound really fun when they first come up, but if you don't think it through, it might not turn out so well." For instance, Day recalls a day at the rental barn after he'd become a good rider and wanted to show off to the guest riders.

He had watched a western movie and the cowboy rode his horse under a limb, then grabbed the limb and swung up on it. "They had a rail used to close the barn door. I thought it'd be really cool to canter in there and grab hold of that rail in front of all of those girls." It was a painful lesson. "I remember reaching up for the rail, and as soon as my feet went straight, my hands came out and it looked like I was suspended in the air."

Day fell on his back, "and the air came out of my lungs." Ms. Jewel saw the whole thing. She walked over and asked, "What did you learn from that?" Day was embarrassed and gasping for air. She said, "Your horse is here to get food. He's going into the stall. You're here showing off. The horse could care less what you're trying to do. He wants to go get fed."

Sonny Boy, "at first terrified me, not meaning to. I didn't even know he could walk for a while because he was always in his truck," said Day.

Like most people who spent any extended time around him, young Lance saw firsthand two different sides of Sonny Boy. "He was laid back when he needed to be, but there was a different side to him as well. I saw that one day."

Ms. Jewel had rules at the rental barn. One of utmost importance: riders cannot run the horses. Most of the rental rides are in the heat of Florida's summer days. If the horses are run, they get overheated and lather up. That means they are taken out of the line, and you can't ride them for the rest of the day. Ms. Jewel always told the riders if they ran a horse, she would charge them double.

"I'll never forget, these guys came out there and they'd been drinking, or maybe they took alcohol and started drinking on the trail," Day said. When they returned to the barn, the horses were all lathered up. Ms. Jewel said, "I told y'all if you run the horses, it will be double. I can't rent those horses out."

"The guy started arguing that he wasn't paying double, and he started cussing. He was cussing and raising a lot of cane in front of the other customers." Ms. Jewel walked over to the barn phone. "You could hear the phone ring at the house. She said, 'I need you down here.' The screen door to the house swung open and Sonny Boy walked down. He had his big hat on."

The abusive customer didn't see Sonny Boy walking through the middle of the barn. "He was just showing himself, being an ass, and still cussing. Sonny Boy walked up to him, hit him one time in the jaw, and knocked him on the ground."

Still sitting on his butt where he'd landed, Day said the guy looked up at Sonny Boy and asked, "You do that to all your customers?"

"No," said Sonny Boy. "Just the ones that cuss at my wife and run my horses." Then, Sonny Boy, "turned around just as calm as he'd come down and he walked back up to the house. You could have heard a pin drop out there."

A couple of weeks later, the man returned and apologized to Jewel and Sonny Boy and said he was wrong. "Again, I saw a different side of Sonny Boy. Sonny Boy let this man out of his corner. He could have pushed it and told him to never come back on the property. But the guy apologized, and Sonny Boy accepted it. He said, 'We're done. We're fine. You know what you did was wrong and I'm over it."

# Sonny Boy and Jim Kittrell: the "Hatfields and McCoys"

*"There was not more than a couple of passes and he was laying on the ground in this little ditch. Sonny Boy was very heavy in those days. I was on top of him all the time. I went to work on his face and his head. I beat him pretty bad."*

**By most any** description, Jim Kittrell has always been a big man. He's what you would call a "presence," one of those guys who stands out in a crowded room. In his younger years, the 83-year-old Kittrell was a tall, rugged man with large hands from working with horses and cows.

When Jim Kittrell spoke, most people listened to what he had to say.

Like Sonny Boy Griffin, who was about four years older, Kittrell had a westside reputation as a hard worker, hard drinker, and hard fighter.

It was well known in west Jacksonville that the two men really didn't care for each other. They first met at the stockyard on Halsema Road, where Kittrell worked one day a week to help a friend. Sonny Boy and Jewel had cows, and Kittrell said Sonny Boy "was always at the sale."

"We didn't really meet," recalled Kittrell. "He just wound up knowing the people I knew. I heard the rumors about him, and I reckon he might have heard the rumors about me. I heard he liked to fight, he liked to drink and get drunk. And I wasn't far from the same. We didn't dodge each other, but we didn't pat each other on the back."

On one of those days Kittrell was working at the stockyard, he and his buddy, Ray Waldrop, went to Baldwin for lunch. After lunch, they drove to a liquor store for something to drink when the stockyard closed at the end of the day.

Kittrell and Waldrop went to the drive thru. Afterwards, instead of heading back to the stockyard, "We pulled around to the side into the grass, got out of the truck, and opened the bottle to take a drink."

About that time, Sonny Boy drove up. Kittrell and Waldrop got out. "We leaned up against the truck to talk a good long time, maybe an hour."

It didn't take long for the liquor to turn their friendly talking into a testosterone test between Sonny Boy and Waldrop. "The words got kind of dry. They was gonna fight," said Kittrell. "I said, 'No. You ain't fighting here. I ain't going to jail.'"

Kittrell told the two men to get in the truck. "Let's go down 301 somewhere down in the woods," he said. When Kittrell reached his destination, the gates were locked to the timber land where they planned to fight. Sonny Boy and Waldrop climbed over the gate. Kittrell followed behind them.

According to Kittrell, Sonny Boy and Waldrop just "walked around and around, blowing like two old bulls. But they wasn't touching each other. I got tired of waiting, and said, 'Come on y'all. You ain't gonna fight. You're chickens, both of you.'"

At that moment, Sonny Boy turned his attention from Waldrop to Kittrell. "Sonny Boy reached up and pulled me around to his face by my shoulder."

Sonny Boy said, "You want some of it?"

"I believe I do," Kittrell replied.

Kittrell said he doesn't know if Sonny Boy ever landed a blow. "There was not more than a couple of passes and he was laying on the ground in this little ditch. Sonny Boy was very heavy in those days. I was on top of him all the time. I went to work on his face and his head," said Kittrell. "I beat him pretty bad."

The three men got back into the truck and returned Sonny Boy to the liquor store. "He went home, and we went back to the stockyard."

The next day, Kittrell brought Sonny Boy's teeth back to him, according to Sonny Boy's son, Michael.

It may be the only fight Sonny Boy lost.

Kittrell's daughter, Galynna, said, "They were like the Hatfields and McCoys."

In a strange twist of fate, Galynna married Sonny Boy's son, Michael, when the two were just teenagers. "Deep down, daddy loved Sonny Boy. As they grew as a family, they didn't have a choice, really."

The two men drank and fought, "for recreation," said Galynna. "It scared us. It worried us because we didn't want our families to be torn

*Rivals Sonny Boy and Jim Kittrell became family when*
*Michael Griffin and Galynna Kittrell married*

up. They were both so hardheaded. It was their way or the highway. They both wanted it their way."

"They were such enemies," said Sonny Boy's wife, Jewel. "They both drank."

Over time, Galynna said the two men grew to respect each other.

Neither Kittrell nor Sonny Boy had a high school education. "They were big, bold men. They lived through a lot of hard times. They scrapped and scraped to get what they had. Both of them were multi-taskers, hard workers."

Like Sonny Boy, Kittrell was always looking for ways to make money. He and his wife, Louise, started the Circle R Riding Stables, which put Kittrell in direct competition with the Griffins.

"We both rented horses," said Jewel Griffin. "He'd see me and ask if I couldn't raise my prices some."

Kittrell recalls it a little different. "I was selling horses, swapping cows, anything, and I got into the same business they was in, renting horses. I can't remember the prices, but I think Jewel was charging $3 an hour. I can't remember," he said. "But I undercut her a dollar. That didn't sit really well out there."

Despite the tension between their fathers, Galynna Kittrell and Michael Griffin, who met at a school dance, decided to date.

Like Michael, Galynna was raised on her parents' ranch. She worked in the family business at Circle R Riding Stables from a young age, buying, selling and trading horses and cows. She also worked at her parents' businesses, Circle K Feed and Circle K Furniture.

Galynna's love for horses and competition rivaled Michael's. She showed pleasure horses and ran barrels. Later, she and Michael competed in team roping and riding cutting horses.

Young Galynna took Michael to the Kittrell barn to meet her dad.

"He had hair halfway down his back and he looked like a buffalo or something. I didn't like it too good, but I didn't have too much to say about it until I found out who he was," said Kittrell.

Kittrell asked Michael if he had a job. Michael said he did.

Kittrell asked who he worked for. Michael replied he worked for his dad.

"Your daddy don't pay you enough to get a haircut?"

"Yes sir."

"Well, you can't come here without one," Kittrell told the Griffin boy. "Has your momma and daddy tried to get you to get a haircut?"

"No."

"Well, they're fixing to now because I'm taking you home."

Kittrell and Michael got into Kittrell's truck and drove to Diamond D. Before getting out to talk to Sonny Boy, Kittrell stuck his pistol in the back of his belt. "If Sonny Boy didn't like what I was saying, I might could have kept him off me," he said.

Michael Griffin got his hair cut that same day.

Michael said while he was dating Kittrell's daughter, "He never talked to me. Every time he saw me, he said something tough."

When Michael got his driver's license, he drove his pickup truck to the Kittrell's to get Galynna. Kittrell, Michael recalls, "was about drunk."

"Where y'all going?"

Michael said they were going to a movie and get something to eat.

"How much money you got?"

Michael told him $20. "It was enough."

Kittrell reached into his pocket and peeled off a hundred-dollar bill.

"Let me tell you something," he said. "If you're going to come and date my daughter, have enough money on you."

"Oh man. He made me so mad I could spit," said Michael. "I put that $100 in my pocket and I was going to spend it. Galynna wouldn't let me."

When 16-year-old Galynna and 17-year-old Michael decided to get married before graduating high school, it fell to Michael to speak with both his dad and his future father-in-law. Michael was a rising senior at Baldwin High School. Galynna was also a senior at Edward H. White High School.

After he spoke with Kittrell, Michael and his future father-in-law got into Kittrell's truck and drove to Diamond D to talk to Sonny Boy. Before getting out of the truck, Kittrell stuck his pistol in the back of his belt. "If Sonny Boy didn't like what I was saying, I might could have kept him off me," he said.

Many years after the iconic fist fight when Kittrell whipped Sonny Boy, they had a second legendary battle that involved gun shots.

One Sunday morning, Sonny Boy phoned Kittrell to ask if he had any liquor. Kittrell responded that he was out. Because the liquor stores in Jacksonville were closed on Sunday, "we decided to go to Callahan where we could buy it after 1 p.m.," Kittrell said.

At the time, the Kittrells lived at Owens Dairy on Highway US 90.

After getting liquor, the two men drove back to Kittrell's house. Sitting at the kitchen table, "We started drinking all over again," said Kittrell.

"Then, somehow or another there comes that dry spot in the conversation."

Sonny Boy says, "I got my shotgun in the truck. I'm going to kill you."

"Don't you go to the truck," Kittrell warned.

"Yep, I'm gonna get my gun," said Sonny Boy.

He got up and walked out the screen door.

Kittrell always kept a shotgun sitting behind the back door.

Sonny Boy's shotgun was in a rack at the truck, which was legal in those days. "We left them hanging up there to hunt," said Kittrell.

When Sonny Boy opened his truck door, Kittrell was standing on his back porch about ten yards away.

"Sonny Boy, don't get that gun."

Sonny Boy removed the shotgun from the rack.

"When he did, I shot out the front end of his truck. Sonny Boy threw his gun down and began screaming. He was hollering at his truck," said Kittrell.

Kittrell phoned Michael. "You'd better come and get your daddy. I'm going to kill him."

Michael drove to Owens Dairy. When he arrived, Kittrell had a gun on the kitchen table pointed at Sonny Boy.

"He ain't got nerve enough to shoot me," said Sonny Boy. "He's a chicken shit."

Michael was shocked. "Oh my God. What in hell is going on here?"

Sonny Boy continued calling Kittrell names. "Take another drink. Maybe if you get drunk enough you can shoot me."

Kittrell just sat there at the table with the gun.

"That son of a bitch done shot my truck. If I get my hand on that gun, I'm going to show him how to use it. I'm going to shoot that bastard. He ain't got nerve enough to shoot me. Chicken shit."

As this back and forth continued between the two men, Michael moved around the room and managed to retrieve the shotgun from the table. "I took all the damn guns. Jim had one in every corner of the house. I was running around gathering them up and Louise (Kittrell's wife) was giving them to me."

He then drove his dad home.

Looking back on that wild experience, Michael reflected, "The relationship wasn't that bad. When they drank, they would do stupid shit."

# Sonny Boy, the Hunting Guru

---

*"I was pretty healthy at the time, but at the time I got into the chair I got claustrophobia and I couldn't stand it. I sat there for a moment and thought if a turkey came by, I wouldn't be able to get my gun around. He told me to get in it and I had so much respect for him I was skittish about getting down."*

**IF YOU KNEW** Sonny Boy Griffin, there's a good chance you hunted with him, and most likely belonged to one of the three hunt clubs he headed over the years.

Those who were young and wanted to learn how to shoot deer and turkeys had a mentor in Sonny Boy. To him, his granddaughters hunted just as good as his grandsons, primarily because he taught them all.

"I started hunting with him when I was five," said granddaughter Jodi Griffin Coxwell, who shot her first deer in the sixth grade.

*Sonny Boy with his dogs after a deer hunt*

"Big Daddy loved turkey hunting. That's a love that me and him shared," said granddaughter K'Leigh Griffin Combs. "He would always tell me, 'If you just sit there and call, that turkey would come around to you.'"

Sonny Boy was always proud when grandchildren killed a deer or turkey. "Any time I killed something. I'd bring him and Granny half of it. He might not always want it, but when I showed it to him it would mean the world to him," K'Leigh said.

"My grandpa was with me the day I killed my first deer," remembered oldest grandson Marty Higdon. "It was the Friday after Thanksgiving in 1982 and I was eleven years old."

The land Sonny Boy, his pals, and members of his family had to hunt on was massive. In the beginning, they leased wooded land owned by nearby Gilman Paper Company, purchasing permits for $40 each year that allowed them to hunt from November until January.

"You could hunt every day, and you could run a truck out of gas and never cover half the roads," said Michael.

"Back then it was open country," said Sonny Boy's friend Dwayne Addy. "We'd start at three o'clock in the morning trying to find where the deer was. If you didn't get there early to find your sign, the other group would find it and beat you to the deer."

Yellow Water Hunt Club had 15,000 acres, part of it behind Diamond D Ranch.

"Daddy was president of the club for years," said son Michael.

Hunt Clubs were the center of activity, where the hunters gathered early before going out, then returned after hunting to sit around a fire, drink and tell stories.

"There was some of them that liked to hit the bottle a little bit," said hunter Bo Padgett. "After we got through hunting, we'd gather around and start telling stories. That's where I learned a lot about my family. Sonny Boy knew my grandma and grandpa and my aunts and uncles."

All of the hunters had CB radios in their trucks so they could be in constant communication. Each had a handle, normally assigned by Sonny Boy, like Wiper Man, Railroad Man, and Blueberry Man.

Sonny Boy's best friend, Donald Wynn, always cooked for the hunt clubs, and was the cook at most all of the Griffin functions like political rallies and family gatherings. Generally, at some point during a hunt party or barbecue hosted by the Griffins where Wynn was cooking, Sonny Boy would sing his favorite song, "Roll Me Over in the

Clover." It brought him and his guests great joy when he sang:

*"Oh, this is number one, And the fun has just begun. Roll me over, lay me down and do it again."*

The chorus would follow:

*"Roll me over in the clover, Roll me over, lay me down And do it again."*

Donald Wynn's handle was Feed Man. Most thought it was because of his cooking.

His son, Donnie Wynn, started hunting with Sonny Boy and his dad when he was six-years-old. He said his father's handle Feed Man was for another reason. "It was because he was in the feed business for thirty years. When he was young, his handle was Pole Cat because he was by himself most of the time. They called him the Lonesome Pole Cat."

His oldest child, daughter Patricia Griffin Wright, only went hunting with her dad once. "He told me I talked too much. I interfered with his hunting." Patricia said they were at the hunt club at Fiftone in Maxwell. "I wanted to talk on the radio to all the guys he was hunting with, and he kept taking the radio away from me."

Sonny Boy, his friends all said, was a great hunter. He knew every inch of the woods. "I idolized him because he was the guru of hunting," said his friend Stewart Dowless. "There wasn't much he didn't know about hunting."

Sonny Boy had a special relationship with his dogs. "He loved the sounds of the dogs," said Padgett.

Lifelong friend Richard Altman grew up with Sonny Boy. "To me, he was a typical dog owner. He'd rather hear the dogs bark than shoot a deer," said Altman. "Matter of fact, he probably didn't shoot many deer in his last twenty years of hunting. All he really enjoyed was being with all the guys and listening to the dogs chase."

During the chase, Sonny Boy was able to know which dog was in front, which dog was in the middle, and which one was in the rear by listening to the barks. "I could never figure that out," Altman said.

"You had to load his dogs up every morning at the same time," said son-in-law Jerry Jordan. "You'd have to put the collars on so tight you couldn't get your finger under it."

Often, Sonny Boy would take five to ten dogs with him.

Sometimes, said Altman, the hunters spent more time hunting the dogs than hunting the deer. "He was always afraid they were going to get out and go over to Cecil Field or somewhere we weren't supposed to be. Sometimes they'd end up all the way down at Middleburg by going through Jennings Forest.

When Sonny Boy got ready to find his dogs that were running in the woods, he had a special trick. "He had a little wand he held out. It had an antenna and all of the dog collars had magnets." Jordan said Sonny Boy would hold up the antenna to find the strongest signal. "That's where the dogs went," he said.

When you can't find your dogs, Addy said, "He taught me how to just take off your shirt and lay it right there in the bushes. When you come back tomorrow that dog will be hanging around your clothes somewhere."

"Everybody wanted Big Daddy's dogs, but he would rarely sell them," said granddaughter Jodi. "If you couldn't find them, he was at the dog pen."

"He used to brag about his dogs. He had some great ones," said Altman.

"Everybody that hunted with him met up where his dog pen was," said Padgett.

Dowless, a retired schoolteacher, said Sonny Boy took a special liking to him and his friend retired coach Danny Dower. "They let us hunt turkey out there. I don't think they let anybody else. The few years as Danny and I got older, they told us to go any time we wanted to, just let them know we were going. We'd go during the week," he said, not wanting to interfere with those hunting on weekends.

Once, Sonny Boy told Dowless and Dower to go out late in the afternoon to a hayfield that was a prime place to hunt turkey. "He said for us to put all our stuff out, then go back out early next morning with no lights on." At first, Dowless said the two men hesitated. Later, "We went out there and set up our stuff on both ends of the hayfield like we were supposed to."

The next morning, Dowless and Dower returned to the hayfield. "Turkeys were all over the field." Both bagged a turkey.

On another occasion, Dowless said Sonny Boy took him to the hayfield and told him to climb up to a stand that was about fifteen feet off the ground. "Stewart, you get up there and the turkeys will come in here." Dowless followed his instructions and climbed the steps up to the box.

"I was pretty healthy at the time, but at the time I got into the chair I got claustrophobia and I couldn't stand it. I sat there for a moment and thought if a turkey came by, I wouldn't be able to get my gun around." Dowless said he faced a dilemma. "He told me to get in it and I had so much respect for him I was skittish about getting down."

After a while, Dowless said he climbed down. "I never did tell him I didn't sit in the stand because he wouldn't have like that a bit." Besides, Dowless said in retrospect, "I thought it was illegal. I don't think you can shoot turkeys out of a stand."

Sonny Boy often lectured hunters on the proper way to call a turkey. Dowless was no exception. "Stewart, you got no business calling so much," he barked. "All you need to do is yell one or two times and the turkey will know where you are. Then, you shut up."

Dowless said Sonny Boy told his hunting buddies about Dowless and Dower. "Well, those two fellas are the nicest people you ever met in your life, salt of the earth people. But they are the sorriest turkey hunters I ever saw."

Normally, a day of hunting was followed by eating, and often drinking.

One day, Sonny Boy and his friend Don Hicks, known as Bread Man, hunted all day at Fifton off Highway 301 near Baldwin. Afterwards, they decided to get something to eat at the new MacDonald's that had recently opened in Baldwin.

When the men reached the MacDonald's drive thru, because Sonny Boy couldn't read, he asked Hicks what they should order. "It's a hamburger joint," he said, "so what they got?"

"Well, let's see," said Hicks, looking at the menu board. "It says here they got something called a Happy Meal that comes with a hamburger and a drink."

"Well, that sounds good. Let's just get us a Happy Meal." Hicks ordered two.

When the two men, who both weighed well north of two hundred pounds, pulled up to the drive thru window, the two women working there were giggling. Sonny Boy and Hicks thought the women were flirting, not knowing that instead, the women were having a big laugh.

When Sonny Boy opened his bag and saw the small hamburger, he said, "What kind of hamburger is this? And look. We got a little toy, too."

# COMMON SENSE BETTER
# THAN BOOK LEARNING

*"We used to ride on the hood of the truck and look for
deer tracks. It would be freezing. When we'd see some
tracks, Sonny Boy would slam on the brakes and throw us
off the hood and it would hurt because it was so cold."*

BO PADGETT, SIXTY-FIVE, and Dwayne Addy, sixty-seven, grew up on
Jacksonville's westside within the shadow of Diamond D Ranch. Their
dads and Sonny Boy Griffin were close friends since childhood.

They hunted together, worked cows, and made moonshine. It was a
friendship as rich as farm dirt.

"My daddy knew Sonny Boy before I was born," said Padgett. "They
was raised up around the same places. They made moonshine together
when they was teenagers."

"We were raised down there where the Herlong Airport is now on what
is Oxbow Road," said Addy. "My dad and Sonny Boy had been friends

since they was young'uns. I got to know Sonny Boy when I was real little."

Both the Addy and Padgett boys started hunting with Sonny Boy when they were ten or eleven years old. "I mainly hung around him to hunt," said Addy.

Often, Bo Padgett would go with the Griffin's son, Michael, during deer season.

Before dawn broke, he remembers, "We used to ride on the hood of the truck and look for deer tracks. It would be freezing. When we'd see some tracks, Sonny Boy would slam on the brakes and throw us off the hood and it would hurt because it was so cold."

Sonny Boy would check the tracks to see if they were large enough to be a buck deer. "If they was big enough to be a buck, he'd mark them, and we'd go look for some more." This went on until daylight.

When the sun came up through the forest trees, Sonny Boy would decide which tracks, "to put the dogs on. He was the hunt master. The dogs would trail the deer and jump them. Then the race was on," Bo said.

"Sonny Boy was like a second daddy to me," said Dwayne. "He taught me everything about a dog, a hound; about how to run a deer and a fox."

His dad, Bobby Addy, jokingly called Sonny Boy, "Fat Boy," said Dwayne.

When he was about ten, young Dwayne went with Sonny Boy and his dad to hunt deer on horseback. "I rode on the back of my dad's horse." They carried the horses to the forest in the back of a pickup truck.

By about two o'clock in the afternoon, Dwayne said, "Not much was going on." Sonny Boy and his dad took a break from hunting to get something to drink. They drove to Lloyd's, the nearest liquor store in Baldwin, about four miles away.

Before they left the forest, Sonny Boy tied his horse, Dollar, to a tree. "My daddy's horse was Cairo, and you couldn't tie him up because he'd just rub his bridle off." When Buddy Addy tied Cairo to the tree anyway, Sonny Boy said, 'Bobby, you know when we get back that horse ain't gonna be there.'"

Dwayne's dad replied, "He'll be right here. He won't be far. He'll be here grazing." They made a friendly wager.

When they finished drinking, the two men and the boy drove back to the woods where they'd left the horses. "When we got back, Sonny Boy had lost his money because the old Palomino horse, Cairo, was right there."

Bobby Addy was "a cutter," like Sonny Boy, Dwayne said. "I thought you knew horses, but Fat Boy, you don't know nothing," his dad quipped.

While Sonny Boy had little education, Dwayne said he was loaded with common sense. "We had a hunt club behind his house called the Yellow Water Hunt Club in Jennings Forest. I went in there to catch some dogs, and I seen where something had drug itself across the dirt road." There was only about forty- minutes of daylight left, so Addy said he called Sonny Boy on his CB. "Come over here and tell me what this is."

When Sonny Boy arrived at the place on the dirt road, he said, "I don't know. Something dragged itself across there."

"I can tell that," Addy retorted.

There were no claw or feet marks. The two hunters went into some nearby bushes. "It's a hog. Somebody must have shot the rear end out of this hog," said Sonny Boy.

By then, the two men had walked almost a mile into the woods. It was getting dark, so they started back. "Hey, we done been by here one time," twenty-year-old Dwayne said as they walked by familiar palmetto bushes and a downed tree.

"All right," said Sonny Boy. "I wish we had a beer."

"Why do you want that?" asked Addy.

"Because we're gonna sit right here."

"What do you mean, we're gonna sit right here?"

"Them dogs are out there in the truck. They're hot and tired from being out here all day, and in a few minutes, they'll go to fighting in that box. When they go to fighting, we'll hear them fighting, and we'll go to them."

The two lost hunters sat there about fifteen minutes when the dogs started barking and fighting, just as Sonny Boy predicted. "He hit the nail on the head. It brought us out of there. He just had more common sense than just about anybody I ever seen."

When they hunted for the hound dogs and couldn't find them, Dwayne said Sonny Boy taught him a trick that always worked. "He told me to just take off my shirt and lay it right in the bushes. 'When you come back tomorrow, that dog will be hanging around your clothes. We go out there and pen dogs every day. They know your scent.'"

In addition to his common sense, Sonny Boy was very quick witted, said Bo. "He could remember everything, and it seemed he always had a comeback. If somebody tried to get something on him, he could come back with something else."

Bo remembers one of those occasions after a hunt when everyone had gathered around the fire to swap stories. "Sonny Boy had quit smoking, but after drinking a few beers he wanted a cigarette. He told Denny Whitehead to give him one."

Whitehead handed Sonny Boy a smoke. "Sonny Boy felt round in his pockets, but he didn't have no lighter. So, he told Denny to give him a light."

Whitehead said, "You ain't got a light?"

"I ain't got nothing but the habit," replied Sonny Boy.

Sitting around a fire at the hunt camps after the day's hunt had ended was one of Bo's favorite times with Sonny Boy. "There was some of the guys who liked hitting the bottle a little bit," he said. "After we got through hunting, we'd gather around and start telling stories. That's when I learned a lot about my family."

Sonny Boy knew Bo's grandparents, as well as his aunts and uncles. "So, he'd start telling stories about them growing up."

Often, the hunt trips were on horseback.

"We would meet up at my grandma and grandpa's house, and she would cook breakfast." His grandmother made large biscuits. "I called them 'cat head biscuits,' because they were so thick," said Bo.

After breakfast, Padgett's grandmother filled empty lard cans with biscuits, Great Northern Beans, rice, "and whatever meat they had," so the guys would have something to eat when they finished hunting at the end of the day.

Bobby Addy "was a scrapper" like Sonny Boy, said Dwayne.

When Sonny Boy Griffin and Bobby Addy were young men, "the police didn't bother you much like they do with drinking these days," said Dwayne. "There was a bar called the Hilltop off Normandy Blvd., where the Wal-Mart is now. When we was kids, that's where they'd all meet up and have a few drinks."

Dwayne was often with his dad on these bar visits. He would be left in the truck when the guys went inside. "They might be in there an hour, and they might be there all day. Every now and then, they would bring us a bag of potato chips or something."

Addy says he can recall an afternoon fight at the Hilltop when he was about twelve. "I remember Sonny Boy out there, and they had knives pulled. Sonny Boy cut the other guy, and the other guy cut Sonny Boy. Sonny Boy got cut pretty good on that deal. Daddy loaded him in the truck and drove him to the hospital."

The County Line Bar near Diamond D Ranch on Highway 301 was another drinking haunt for Sonny Boy and his pals. Dwayne, who started with his dad to bars at an early age, became a regular drinking companion of Sonny Boy's as an adult.

"It was around 1983 and Sonny Boy had just bought him a brand-new Chevrolet truck. I had just bought one too, except his was diesel and mine was gas," said Dwayne, whose CB handle was J.J. "We got in the bar drinking and messing around," when Sonny Boy said, "J.J., I bet that Chevy I just bought with that diesel will out pull that gas one." J.J. said, "I don't think so."

By then, Addy said the two men had been drinking most of the day. They went out into the parking lot and hooked their trucks together at the front bumpers with a chain. "So, we go to tugging on one another. He pulled me a little bit and I'd pull him a little bit." Sonny Boy finally decided he'd had enough. "We done pulled both of the bumpers out on the two trucks."

Sonny Boy had gotten out of his truck, but his door was wide open. "I mashed on the gas again and hit his door. It knocked him down. It's a wonder his truck didn't run over him." Sonny Boy cussed Dwayne and told him how stupid he was. "We dusted him off and went back in the bar to drink some more."

Sonny Boy always gave his hunting buddies—and most everyone else—a nickname. "One day, I was in the woods with Sonny Boy and two other guys that hunted with us all the time," J.J. said. "One was Railroad Man, and the other they called Clyde Crook." The other three men had been at the hunt camp all night. They had pretty good hang overs when I drove up there about eleven o'clock."

Addy said the three men were sitting outside their trucks, "letting the sun hit on them."

Finally, Sonny Boy spoke up. "Clyde," he said. "Ya'll believe in God?" Railroad Man didn't answer. Clyde said, "Yea, I believe in Him."

"Well, tell me this," Sonny Boy started. Before he could finish, Railroad Man said, "Clyde, you'd better get your thinking cap on because he's gonna come with a good one."

Then, Sonny Boy said, "You know, they say when you die and you go to heaven, you don't want for nothing."

"Yea, that's what we hear," said Clyde.

"What do you reckon that means? You just find you an old stump up there and you just twiddle your thumbs?"

Then, Sonny Boy repeated, "It says you don't want for nothing. That's a powerful word, that word 'Nothing.'"

# Scaring the Booze
# Out of Sonny Boy

———— ᔍᔍ ————

*"I'm a normal person. But you know, I found out real
fast it was better to keep my mouth shut, go to bed, and
discuss it in the morning. You can't argue with a drunk.
I learned really fast that now is not the time to protest."*

**OVER THE FIRST** two decades of the Griffin's marriage, Sonny Boy had a
well-earned reputation as a fun-loving, hard-drinking, and sometimes
hotheaded rounder who would fight at the drop of a hat after boozing
it with his hunting pals.

By all accounts, after drinking, Sonny Boy could be like a wild cowboy
out of an old western movie.

"Uncle Sonny Boy wanted to get out and drink with his buddies," said
nephew Terrance Freeman. "At times, he could not be a pleasant person
to be around. Aunt Jewel is a little bit of a saint for being able to handle
all of that."

Many of their friends and family members often wondered just why Jewel did put up with his bad behavior. "She couldn't keep him in line. Nobody could keep Sonny Boy in line. Sonny Boy did what Sonny Boy wanted to do," said his close friend Charles Spencer.

It was an opinion shared by many people in the Griffin family circle.

Sonny Boy and Jewel's oldest child, Patricia Wright, remembers what it was like on occasions when her daddy would come home drunk. Sonny Boy, she said, "was a good father," but things could be tense. "I would get in between them," she recalled.

She said as a ten-year-old, "I begged my mother to divorce him. But she said, 'Patricia if I divorce your daddy, I wouldn't have anything. I love your daddy. I can't divorce him.'"

"I'm glad she didn't," said Patricia.

One day, when her granddaughter, Tiffany Williamson, was driving Jewel to a doctor's appointment, she said her grandmother told her of the time she really did leave Sonny Boy. "She said Big Daddy messed up and went off with some hunting buddies and drinking."

Jewel said she was not pleased when Sonny Boy would come home drunk. "I'm a normal person. But you know, I found out real fast it was better to keep my mouth shut, go to bed, and discuss it in the morning. You can't argue with a drunk. I learned really fast that now is not the time to protest."

Jewel said she thought about leaving Sonny Boy while her four children were young. "But where you gonna go with four kids? Whose doorstep are you going to park on with four kids."

It was only when Sonny Boy was drinking "that he was belligerent, and he could come home raising hell. I prayed about it hard." But she said she would always forgive Sonny Boy and "let it go."

Finally, Jewel had enough. Now that her four children were grown and out of the house, she made a plan.

"He come home one night drunk. Oh my God, he was raising hell. He threatened to beat me up."

Jewel was ready. A month earlier, when Sonny Boy had shown the same behavior, she started preparing for her getaway the next time it happened again. She had stored some clothes and money in her van.

"When he went to sleep, I left." She secretly drove to her younger sister Neni Jenkins farm near Gainesville. Jewel didn't tell any of her children she was leaving. "I told my sister, 'If he calls here about me, tell him you have not seen me.'"

After a week, Jewel finally phoned home.

"Where you at?" Sonny Boy asked.

"I'm in Ocala," said Jewel, fibbing. "I got a job up here on this horse farm. I'm coming home to get my clothes, and I'm going back. I don't have to put up with you coming in here drunk anymore. I don't have any kids, and all I got is myself. I don't have to put up with it anymore."

Jewel didn't have a job on a horse farm in Ocala. "But he thought I did."

As Jewel was gathering up her clothes, Sonny Boy promised her he would change. "He said he would never, never do it again."

"Please don't leave."

"I really loved him," said Jewel. "I didn't want to leave."

After she came home, Jewel said, "He never come home drunk again. They had a hunting club, and he would have a couple of beers with the guys, but he never got drunk. No hard liquor."

There is no doubt Sonny Boy wanted Jewel to come back home because he loved and missed her greatly, but she has another thought, as well. "I left him with that barn that he'd never taken care of a day in his life."

# Hog Dogs, Hard Work, and Hell Raising Cowboys

*"The damn horse weren't broke, so I rode him from Sonny Boy's house all the way to Orange Park where we lived. It was twenty hard miles over mule and wagon roads. He was broke by the time I got him home."*

**BROTHERS FRANK AND** Charles Spencer were raised up with Sonny Boy Griffin during the post-Depression hard scrabble days of the late 1930s and 1940s. All three boys had strong, hardworking fathers who expected their sons to work, but also gave them plenty of room to roam free and grow up bare-knuckled in the forest and open spaces of west Jacksonville and neighboring Clay County, where they ran through the woods barefooted, rode horses, fished, and hunted.

"Back in those days we had so much fun. We had horses and work to do. Everybody pitched in. It was a different world," said Frank.

The Spencer children were born in a Clay County log cabin on land that today is a cemetery in back of the Orange Park Mall.

"Life was rough," said Charles Spencer, 84. "We didn't have all the novelties they have now. Back then, children worked to support the family out in the pastures, driving cattle, and whatever. Pappa made sure we stayed busy. There wasn't any money. Mostly what you had was what you lived on."

What the two brothers said they "lived on" were wild hogs. "That's what we ate," said Charles. "We didn't have no refrigerator, no electricity, no running water. Nothing. We just lived in an old shack."

"We'd go out the back door and pull water up out of a well," said Frank. "You didn't have to make a lot to buy groceries because groceries was about $3-$5 a week. Mostly, what we bought was sugar, rice, salt and pepper."

Frank Spencer, 85, described their early years as "very lonesome. Nobody lived within a mile of each other. But we had our brothers and sisters to play with."

When there was no meat, the Spencers would catch and butcher a hog.

"You have two types of hog dogs," said Charles. "One type will trail the hog and bay him up. Bay dogs surround the hog, but they won't bite."

When the bay dogs have a hog cornered, "They make a different sound. That's when you turn the catch dogs loose."

Like the bay dogs, the two catch dogs also work as a team. One dog will grab an ear and the other dog will grab the hog's other ear. "He's caught right there. Then, you just walk up and grab him behind the back legs and throw him over, put your knee on his neck, and tie him up. It was kind of rough."

There were also steers to butcher, which is how the Spencer boys really got to know young Sonny Boy Griffin. Starting when he was six years old, Sonny Boy went once a week with his dad, Dewey, to the Spencers to butcher steers for Mr. Griffin's meat market. "He would buy beef from my daddy," said Charles.

"His daddy and my daddy would kill three or four steers and butcher them," said Frank. "Me and Sonny Boy would cut palmetto fans to lay in the back of the truck. That way, when they got through butchering the cows, they could lay the meat on the palmetto fans so it wouldn't get dirty. After you laid the meat on it, you covered the meat with another layer of palmetto fans and put a piece of fat lighter on top to keep the palmetto fans from blowing off."

"They didn't have a Food and Drug Administration back then," Charles said.

By the time the Spencers and Sonny Boy were in their early teens, they were unafraid, expert, and sometimes foolish, cowboys. They loved to rope cows.

"Sonny Boy was a good cowboy," said Charles. "He could rope better than Frank and me."

Frank, however, says he was a better horseman than Sonny Boy. "I broke people's horses for them when I was young. I was always driving cattle, and there weren't no cutting horses back then."

Once, the Spencer's dad and Sonny Boy went together to a horse sale in Georgia. Sonny Boy hauled a newly bought horse back to Diamond D. "The next morning, my daddy said, 'I bought you a horse. We got to go get him.'"

Frank was told to ride the horse home from Diamond D. "The damn horse weren't broke, so I rode him from Sonny Boy's house all the way to Orange Park where we lived. It was twenty hard miles over mule and wagon roads. He was broke by the time I got him home."

Jewel Griffin, Sonny Boy, and the Spencer brothers also raced horses. "One day, Sonny Boy told me he had just bought a racehorse, a stud named Whiskey," said Charles. "He was fast. Jewel raced him and she said, 'If you want to ride a fast horse, get on him. That's the fastest horse I've ever been on.'"

Whiskey became Jewel's racehorse, a money winner most every time he ran.

"I remember one day I was riding him, and we were running down a dirt road. There was a bridge about half a mile in front, and I was worried if I was going to be able to stop before I got to the bridge. He would have killed me," said Charles. "I'm telling you he was like lightening. He probably outrun every horse in this part of the country."

Sonny Boy also used Whiskey to drive cows. "One day he took him into Yellow Water Creek. The creek had steep banks on it and the horse couldn't get out. He drowned."

In those days, Sonny Boy and the Spencer brothers didn't buy their ropes.

Cecil Field, a large naval air base, dominated much of west Jacksonville. The base was a dozen miles by horseback from the Spencer's place in Orange Park.

To train new pilots during World War II, military planes often took target practice at Cecil. "They would pull these targets, like a flag, about quarter of a mile behind a plane," remembers Charles. "The target would be tied to a nylon rope that was tied to the plane."

The plane carrying the target behind it, "would fly up into the air and the other plane would come behind it and shoot the flag." Normally, the pilot would hit the target. On those occasions when the pilot missed and instead shot the nylon rope, cutting it free, "we'd go out and pick up the rope," said Charles.

Often, the boys used the rope they had secured at Cecil Field to tie up hogs to their saddles to bring home. "We'd throw the hog on the saddle, then we got behind the saddle and rode home. We didn't shoot hogs. We'd catch them, bring them home, and fatten them up," said Charles.

They also used their ropes to hunt cows over long distances, sometimes riding from Clay Hill to Orange Park and Orange Park to Cecil Field. "We cow hunted all over this part of the country," said Charles.

"Our daddy and us drove our 200-300 cows from Cecil Field almost to Blanding Blvd. Back then, it was free open range." Usually, said Charles, there would be four to five cowboys and two or three good dogs on the cattle drives.

The Spencers marked their cows with the brand Anchor Three (the cross of Jesus, Father, Son and Holy Spirit).

"Whenever somebody would lose a cow, we'd all go hunting it. Sometimes we found it, sometimes we didn't."

On occasion, neighbors had to help the Spencers find some of their cows because Sonny Boy cut their fence wire.

"After the fence law come in, we leased 28,000 acres from Towers Hardware. My fence kept getting cut," said Frank. Somebody, he said, would come on the property in a truck and ride around. The next morning, Frank would discover his cows were out.

"I got tired of having to get up on Sunday morning, go hunt cows, put them back in, and fix the fence."

Frank decided it was time to act. "I got me some one-inch pipe about a foot long. I cut it with a hack saw on an angle to make it real sharp. Whoever was cutting the fence was doing it in the same place every time. "So, I went about ten feet from where they cut the fence and I drove the pipes in the ground, leaving the sharp end up."

It worked.

"Well, I got a phone call Saturday night about 12 o'clock. It was Sonny Boy, and he was drunk. He went in there and it had flattened all four of his tires."

Turns out, Sonny Boy was night deer hunting on the Spencer's leased land.

"He was drunk as a skunk and told me what he was going to do."

The next morning Frank told his dad about what had happened. "Let's go," his father said. He had his shot gun with him.

They drove to Diamond D. Frank's dad blew the truck horn. "Sonny Boy comes to the door and says, 'Oh, I was drunk as hell, and I didn't mean nothing.'"

Another time, when Sonny Boy had been drinking all day with Frank and Charles, Sonny Boy had a strange idea. "I'd like a piece of tail," he said.

"What kind of tail?" Frank asked.

"Gator tail. Hell, what do you think I'm talking about?"

"I think I know where one usually stays," said Frank.

The three adventurous guys rode to the location and got about 150 yards from where Frank said the gator usually lays beside a log. Charles, the better shot of the brothers, took out his rifle. Frank tells Charles to walk by the log. "When you go by it, he's gonna make a run for the water. You be real quiet and you can get around it and shoot it." Charles walked past the log, but there was no gator.

They walked another fifty yards. "The gator woke up and passed by my brother into the water." Charles fired.

Sonny Boy asked, "You reckon you hit him?"

Frank said, "He shot, didn't he?"

The gator went to the water hole and fell in.

After a while, Sonny Boy said he was going into the water to get the gator. "How big is he?"

"Probably eight or nine feet," said Frank.

Sonny Boy, who was only about a foot taller than the water hole's bank, crawled in. After ten minutes, Frank decided the gator was dead, and he, too, went into the water hole to help.

Frank had cut a 12-foot-long stick and left a limb on the end to use as a hook. "I hooked onto something, so I told Sonny Boy to hold on to the end of the stick. I felt around under the water, and it was a gator."

Frank came back to the surface. "I got him," he said. "Sonny Boy stepped aside four or five feet, and I kept pulling and pulling." Eventually, Frank pulled the gator right in front of Sonny Boy.

"He screamed, threw up both hands, and said, 'I just can't make myself touch him.'"

They put a rope around the gator to pull him out of the water hole.

"Sonny Boy said, 'Somebody's got to help me out.' So, we put the rope around his waist and pulled him out. Sonny Boy was heavier than the gator. He was as round as he was tall."

Sonny Boy, said Charles, often "went into places he shouldn't have to get a little nip."

Cecil Field Naval Station was home to thousands of Navy personnel and operated on thousands of acres of west Jacksonville property. Cecil's sailors often frequented the bars around Diamond D Ranch. "There was a lot of drinking and carrying on, and Sonny Boy would go in there," said Charles.

"I don't know why, but they always thought they were going to whip Sonny Boy. They never whipped him." According to Charles, Sonny Boy would "whip a half dozen of them. It didn't make no difference how many it was, it was just more fun to him."

Sonny Boy was well-known for his big-fisted punch. "When he hits one of them, the first thing that hits the floor is the fella's head. I mean, he was just bad. But he was good. He never really started trouble. He just wouldn't walk away at all."

# BATTLING JACKSONVILLE'S
# POWERFUL TO SAVE THE WESTSIDE

—◦◦◦—

*"I had gotten out on a limb without listening to the
community. I thought, 'Wow, this is great!' I had a governor
who was bullishly pushing it, the seduction of economic
impact, then I had a community that had moved on."*

**PRIOR TO 1999,** Naval Air Station (NAS) Cecil Field, sitting on 17,000
acres, was the elephant in west Jacksonville. The Cecil Field Complex,
which included three additional military facilities, covered another
5,000 westside acres.

The base opened in 1941. Shortly after the Japanese attacked Pearl
Harbor, naval operational support for the war effort began in earnest
at Cecil.

In 1943, Cecil Field became the principal war-at-sea and dive-bomb-
ing training center for the Navy and Marine Corps. And Cecil Field
was known as a pilot's last stop before being sent to war in the Atlantic
or Pacific Fleets.

In the mid-1950s, Cecil Field was one of only four naval air stations selected as Master Jet Bases, meaning their operations included carrier-based jet aircraft.

During its first half-century of operations, most people in Jacksonville, including its westside neighbors, looked at Cecil Field as a driver of the area's economy.

The Griffins and Diamond D Ranch were no exception.

In 1993, the federal Base Realignment and Closure Commission (BRAC) notified the City of Jacksonville that Cecil Field would be shutting down as part of a nationwide base closing initiative. The closure and realignment process was created in 1988 to create more military efficiency and reduce pork barrel politics by members of Congress.

Once the Navy notified the city it was being gifted the base, the city began preparing a reuse plan to develop the base property and facilities for manufacturing and industrial companies.

"When Cecil Field started closing, we were scared to death," said Michael Griffin. "Most of our business had a lot to do with the military. We did squadron parties at the base. We had them board horses out here, and we made good money. Their kids came to ride our rental horses."

Griffin, who has long been active in westside business matters and politics, began attending meetings held by the city to plan and discuss the future of Cecil Field. "The City of Jacksonville got together, and they really had a good plan for what they were going to do at the base. And they had a developer," said Griffin.

Because of the city's aggressive planning, as well as the size and strategic location of the abandoned airbase, Griffin said, "You could see it was going to be nothing but growth."

Instead of opposing the base closure, a lot of westside leaders became involved in the planning process.

By the time of the spring election for mayor in 2003, the redevelopment of Cecil Field was underway. "Grumman was there. Flagstar was there. The community college was there. These were big employers," said Griffin.

In 2002, the Griffin family and other westside influencers like J.B. Coxwell and Jim Kittrell got behind the mayoral candidacy of young John Peyton. While John's father was well-known throughout Jacksonville, the 38-year-old novice candidate had little name recognition or support when he entered the race.

"I remember meeting those families," said Peyton. "I was really taken by their hospitality, their southern charm and how they make you feel right at home. The westside reminds me of a small southern town."

Peyton's campaign reasoned that if his long-shot campaign for mayor had a chance to succeed, he had to have big support in Jacksonville's west and north sides. "Both areas have some very similar qualities."

Because of the strong support he received in the westside from the Griffins and others, Peyton was elected mayor in 2003.

After he was sworn in as mayor, federal base realignment came up again in the public discussion. Gov. Jeb Bush, the Jacksonville Chamber of Commerce, and other business leaders got behind a strong movement to have Cecil re-opened as a Naval base.

"When the new base realignment came up, I was seduced by jobs," reflected the newly elected mayor.

"Jeb Bush was the driving force of returning Cecil Field. He just saw this as the crowning jewel of economic development." After hearing an initial pitch, Peyton said, "It was a no-brainer."

But it wasn't a "no-brainer" for the Griffins and thousands of other families who lived on the westside, watching the economic turnaround at what had become the Cecil Commerce Center.

More important, they no longer had to live with the intrusive, incessant, even abusive noise from the low-flying Navy jets that crisscrossed the westside skies all day long. Westsiders were enjoying the silence while watching new investment and job growth around them.

Bush and Peyton said they would spend $200 million in state and local tax dollars to reopen the base, which would return 244 F/A-18 Super Hornet jets and over 11,000 employees. F/A 18s are known as the military's noisiest airplane at 117 decibels on takeoff and 114 decibels when landing.

It was also predicted that there would be more than 200,000 flights annually from the airfield.

It was estimated that as many as 10,000 residents would fall within Cecil Field's "noise zones."

"I was on all these boards, and I knew what Cecil Field had become," said Michael Griffin. "I knew what was coming down the pike, and what the potential was."

Griffin was a board member of the newly constructed Equestrian Center that was a short distance from Diamond D. "They started talking about doing away with the Equestrian Center."

Michael and others thought Gov. Bush and the city leaders downtown had lost their minds.

After the base closure, homes were built in new neighborhood developments near the Cecil Field property. "If you brought the base back, those houses weren't built for the noise of these jets"

In addition, the county school board had purchased 130 acres for an elementary school, middle school, and high school in the flight's path. That plan wouldn't survive if the jets returned because the schools wouldn't be able to meet sound requirements.

Griffin and other community leaders decided to organize to fight against base re-opening. They formed the Better Westside Project and hired lobbyist and political consultant Alberta Hipps to guide their opposition. She was a former councilmember representing the westside and had been council president that oversaw the 1999 closing.

Hipps also brought in a young public relations consultant, John Daigle, to help.

In the meantime, the mayor named Blue Cross/Blue Shield lobbyist Mike Hightower to lead the effort to bring back the base. Hightower was a high-powered political force in Jacksonville and Tallahassee. He'd also been Peyton's finance chair in his recent campaign.

"We felt we had to be clandestine in everything we did," said Hipps, recognizing the powerful forces on the other side.

"John Coxwell put in $50,000 to help us run it," said Michael. Everybody jumped in."

Meanwhile, Peyton was operating on a false notion that westsiders would be happy for the base to return with its employees and jet airplanes.

"I had remembered about the base closure and how devastating it was," said Peyton. "Everybody said Cecil Field was the heartbeat of the westside. Not being a westsider, that's what I knew."

Hipps said when she phoned the mayor, who she had supported, Peyton pretty much blew her off.

Today, Peyton recognizes how off the mark his thinking was back then. "What I didn't take into account was things had changed on the westside. There was a new westside emerging that was different. It was a tightknit community embracing a new vision."

Three key things then happened that had a huge impact on the future of Cecil Commerce Center.

"I had gotten out on a limb without listening to the community," Peyton confessed. "I thought, 'Wow, this is great!' I had a governor who was bullishly pushing it, the seduction of economic impact, then I had a community that had moved on."

All the while, Peyton was engaged in testifying to bring back the base before BRAC and the Congress. "We were fairly entrenched on the issue," he said.

One day after Peyton had his first public meeting with westside residents and business owners, property owners began receiving letters from the state to buy their property.

As the process evolved, Peyton said a few things started becoming clear to him. "I needed to find out more about what the westside thinks, and I needed to understand where the Navy was. They had been silent on the issue, which really concerned me."

So, he turned to the Griffins.

"I needed to go back and listen to some straight talking. Sonny Boy was the guy."

Peyton encountered the same qualities he saw during his campaign. However, this time, "I got a dose of that on the other side of the coin during Cecil Field."

Peyton had developed a pretty strong opinion about Sonny Boy during his campaign. "He didn't give a rat's ass about what anybody thought about him or anyone else. What you saw was what you got, and he certainly had opinions. I also got the feeling he had great instincts. And he was well-respected."

The mayor took a day off from the office and got into Sonny Boy's truck to visit the Griffin's westside friends and neighbors. "He introduced me to these folks. He said the mayor is here and he wants to hear what you think."

As a result, Peyton said, "Two things happened. Having his introduction helped, and him saying I was there to hear them out helped."

Sonny Boy, said Peyton, "was a man of few words. He really wanted the neighbors to do the talking." Peyton enjoyed Sonny Boy's straight talk when he did say something. "As mayor, often people say what they think you want to hear. I didn't have that problem with Sonny Boy."

"We spent the entire day driving, and I cherish that time."

"They all cussed him and loved him at the same time," said Michael. "He's got thick skin because he took an ass-chewing in several places."

Meanwhile, the Hipps-led group continued meeting privately to plan and organize.

An important City Council committee on the future of Cecil Commerce was meeting. The clock was ticking. The best chance and probably last shot for the Hipps group was coming up.

Hipps and the Better Westside Project held their most important meeting one evening in the bunkhouse at Diamond D.

It was during that meeting when consultant Daigle suggested an outrageous idea that turned out to be genius.

Jacksonville's City Hall sits just across a narrow street from historic Hemming Plaza, one of Jacksonville's best-known parks. Daigle's proposal was to position gigantic loudspeakers strategically in the park, aimed toward City Hall. During the council 2 o'clock committee meeting, the mammoth speakers would blast ear piercing noise that replicated the level of sound of jet engines that westside residents would hear throughout the day if the base returned.

Councilman Lad Daniels was committee chair. "He thought bringing the base back was a great idea," said Hipps.

During the bunkhouse meeting, Hipps was told to attend the council committee meeting. When she heard a blasting sound from outside, she was to walk from her seat to the podium and tell Daniels, "You are about to hear the noise we hear from the Navy Base."

Hipps was unsure about the idea. "I said, 'I don't think we should do that.'" She left the bunkhouse.

The next morning, she received a call from others at the meeting who told her, "You've got to do this. You've got to do your part."

When the jet plane-equivalent blasts burst from the speakers during the meeting, it felt like all of City Hall was shaking. It's a wonder windows didn't shatter.

Members of the Better Westside Project had made their point.

Meanwhile, Peyton's own thinking about the return of the base was changing, and his strategy was evolving.

The mayor called a town meeting inside the Equestrian Center to hear from westside residents. "Seven-hundred people came out and it sent a very loud signal. They feel strong about it."

Peyton had made something clear to members of his staff and others from city government who attended the meeting. "I said we weren't going to leave this place until everybody here has a chance to speak." The meeting ended just before midnight.

Michael recalls the city had "a number of influential people there. No matter how you cussed them, they told you the good that was to come from the base coming back."

Peyton, sitting on a bar stool in the middle of the center, just listened. "John was a good listener," said Michael

"My regret was I didn't do that first," Peyton said. "It would have saved me a lot of headaches."

For Michael, his wife Galynna, sisters Cathy and Tammy, and especially his parents Sonny Boy and Jewel, "It was a fight, but a loving fight. If they brought the base back, it was going to devalue our land. Why devalue what we've held together all these years?"

Today, Cecil Commerce Center is a 17,000-acre commercial and industrial complex. Originally, the goal was to bring a mega-project to the Center. Since then, several major deals have been forged, including an aircraft manufacturing plant for Boeing, a DaimlerChrysler van assembly plant, and a Spirit AeroSystems complex.

In July 2021, the Jacksonville Aviation Authority had a ribbon-cutting ceremony for an 11-story air traffic control tower and spaceflight facility at Cecil Commerce Center.

The new facility is named the Dr. Norman Thagard Mission Control Center. Thagard graduated from the westside's Paxon High School. He completed five space missions, including being the first American astronaut to go to space on a Russian spacecraft.

To help get the spaceport ready for a hoped-for launch by mid-2022, Florida Governor Ron DeSantis announced in November 2021 that to construct new roadway and infrastructure to the aerospace facility, the state was adding $6 million to an existing $4 million the project had received from Florida DOT, and another $3 million from Spaceport Florida

The spaceport's growth, said the governor, "has been an economic engine as aerospace companies are moving in."

An estimated 5,000 employees work at companies like Bridgestone Americas Tire Operation, Flightstar Aircraft Services, Northrop Grumman, Amazon and Pratt & Whitney.

The Center is also home to the Jacksonville Equestrian Center, Cecil Aquatic Center and Florida State Community College at Jacksonville.

# Ranch Grows, Values Remain

*"I love the way we live and make a living. Watching baby calves born, grass grow after you fertilize it, planting trees and coming back twenty years later, harvesting them, and profiting off your labor."*

DIAMOND D RANCH all started in 1954 on forty acres of mostly wooded, hard scrabble land with an old log house that was built in the 1880s. In its first years, Sonny Boy Griffin and his dad, Dewey Griffin, raised cattle and brewed moonshine there to make a living and purchase additional land.

In 1960, Jewel Griffin opened a rental barn with six horses and Diamond D was in business for good.

Over time, the ranch grew to a full-blown cattle operation, horse boarding, meat butchering, rodeos, pony rides and hayrides.

"My dad sold cattle and built every one of these barns," said Sonny Boy's son Michael. "He raised cattle in these woods, and when they wanted to expand the business, he'd sell off cattle and build another part."

His parents were entrepreneurs, he said. "They were always doing things. On Friday nights they had hayrides. You had to get on a wait list," Michael said. The Griffins catered to church groups.

Sonny Boy and Michael had 1,500 hogs. Seven days a week, Michael would wake up at 2 a.m. and often accompanied by Sonny Boy and Jewel's oldest grandson, twelve-year-old Marty Higdon, drive a large stock trailer loaded with 55-gallon drums into Jacksonville to pick up swill for the hogs.

"We'd go out to Moose Haven, the old folks' home, and get all their scraps," said Higdon. "We'd go to a couple of grocery stores, Krispy Kreme donuts, restaurants, nursing homes, anywhere."

Once the swill was back at the ranch around 7 a.m., it was cooked in a cut off water cooler with burners underneath before being fed to the pigs.

Today, Diamond D Ranch is a thriving and successful enterprise that sits on 500 acres in west Jacksonville. It is enjoyed by several thousand children and adults every year.

*Jewel and Sonny Boy in the middle of their large family.*

SONNY BOY AND JEWEL GRIFFIN

The ranch bills itself as a sixth generation working horse and cattle ranch with 100 horses and 600 head of cattle.

But Diamond D is far more than that. In addition to cows and its boarding and horse rental barns, the ranch's reach is wide:

In a partnership with Duval County Public Schools and other organizations, as many as 20,000 school children visit the ranch each year for Diamond D's Educational Field Trips.

Its two boarding barns stay full, housing over 50 horses.

Reservations are required to rent horses for trail rides into the adjacent 25,000-acre Jennings Forest, which is loaded with wildlife and miles of riding trails.

The ranch hosts Family Farm Fun Day so city dwellers can participate in ranch activities and learn the value of farm life.

Twice each year, in the spring and fall, Diamond D hosts Diamonds in the Rust, a three-day vintage market that attracts hundreds of high-end vendors and thousands of people looking for vintage treasures and farmhouse finds.

Each summer Diamond D holds week-long day and overnight camps to teach children about horses and horsemanship. The camps are attended by hundreds of kids and always have a waiting list.

Michael Griffin and his wife Galynna built a beautiful barn pavilion where weddings, corporate and holiday special events are held year-round.

But no matter how the ranch grows and changes, through the sixty-years of its existence, certain principles have remained foundational for Diamond D founders Sonny Boy and Jewel Griffin, and the five generations of Griffins who have followed.

Work hard every day, and when you finish the work, enjoy the results of your labor.

Respect, appreciate and nourish what you have, starting with the land, animals, boarders, customers, and employees that help make it happen.

Be guided by your faith and take care of your family.

"It's being good stewards of the land," said Galynna. "It's a way of life for us."

"I love the way we live and make a living," Michael said. "Watching baby calves born, grass grow after you fertilize it, planting trees and coming back twenty years later, harvesting them, and profiting off your labor."

Each of the ranch's enterprises is highly organized and often very creative. Beyond profit, there are other motivations for what the Griffins do at Diamond D, especially when it comes to the summer camps and other activities that involve children and families.

K'Leigh Griffin Combs, who directs the Educational Field Trips, said it's important for children to learn "how food gets from the farm to the table, and from the pasture to the plate. And it's important for them to learn they are eating the safest food on the planet."

"With the Educational Field Trips and Camps, we want to show that when they make decisions later in life, how hard it is to keep these ranches going," said Michael.

"We felt the need to educate children on the need for ranches," said Galynna. "We are a dying breed. If we don't educate our children, who is going to feed America?"

The Educational Field Trips are held year-round. The field trips are hands on, including feeding cattle and bison, and learning the history of the Florida Cracker cattle and the horse. "They learn Americans need cowboys on a daily basis."

Nature walks teach kids about Northeast Florida's plants and wildlife.

"They ride in the wagon through a herd of cattle and buffalo that come up to the wagon and eat right out of their hands," said Galynna. The children also visit the ranch's petting zoo, and can have pony rides, as well as have fun on a carousel, the Dixie cartwheel, and bounce houses.

The camps began when Michael and Galynna were looking for a way to make income during the summer months when school was out, and families were taking vacations and going to the beach. "Daddy (Jim Kittrell) said we needed to start a summer horse camp. We built the bunkhouse. Our first camp counselors were Jodi and Amy (the two oldest daughters). The horse camps have been going for thirty summers, and they stay full."

*Summer camps are a big part of Diamond D life*

The day camp, which is for boys and girls, is held Monday through Friday. Overnight camps are for girls only. Campers stay overnight in the ranch bunkhouse.

"Participating in a horse camp helps build a kid's self-confidence and good decision-making skills," said Michael. "We promote independence, and they learn responsibility and cooperation, and all we can teach them about a horse in a week."

At the camps, children spend hours in the saddle and participate in demonstrations from vets, trainers and farriers.

The camps also have Bible devotions throughout the week.

The Griffins erected a 40x80 tent to house their special events.

The grand barn pavilion followed. It's where weddings, corporate and special events are held, and it's the site of the two annual Diamond in the Rust vintage markets.

*Pavilion host events all year*

SONNY BOY AND JEWEL GRIFFIN

Galynna grew up in her parent's furniture business, and she developed a talent for home decorating. She recalled, "My Aunt Frances suggested we had the perfect place to hold a vintage market. We were always looking for ways to add to the ranch." Daughter K'Leigh came up with the name of Diamonds in the Rust Vintage Market.

The semiannual vintage market is held the last weekend in March, and the weekend prior to Thanksgiving each year. It attracts large crowds over three days to shop with some of the South's top vendors.

The vendors have great one of a kind finds. "They set up some of the prettiest things you've ever seen," said Galynna, including vintage treasures, farmhouse finds, home décor, re-loved furniture, handcrafted items, and unique relics. "Most of it is handmade, hand painted, and antiques. It's all juried. We want to keep it unique, not like a flea market."

There are also food trucks and Tasty Treats.

Because everything is juried, the Griffins screen vendors so there aren't too many in the same category.

Tickets for patrons are available online as well as the gate for Friday, Saturday, and Sunday.

The Diamond D Ranch barn pavilion has become a favorite location for weddings and receptions.

The two foundational ranch experiences, rental horses, and the boarding barn remain operational and successful after sixty years.

After the rental barn burned, Jewel Griffin decided she didn't want to reopen it. Within two years, Michael and Galynna, who had been promoting pony rides, stepped in, took it over, and built a new riding stable. They called it Diamond D Rent Horse Stables.

*Crowds flock to the vintage market twice a year*

SONNY BOY AND JEWEL GRIFFIN

"That doesn't sound right," Galynna said. "We had Griffin Party Ponies and we weren't just a stable. So, we created our own corporation." Their son-in-law David Coxwell said, "Just call it Diamond D Ranch. Ranch says everything." Thus, was born Diamond D Ranch, Inc. "There are two different entities," said Galynna. "But we're all one big family."

Diamond D Stables, Inc. is Jewel's boarding facility.

Rental trail rides must be reserved in advance. For the one-hour ride, you must be seven years of age or older. Riders for the two-hour trail ride must be ten or older. The half day ride lasts four to five hours.

Family matriarch Jewel first opened the boarding barn in 1960. She remains deeply involved in its daily operations and in the lives of her boarders.

At one time, she had eighty-four boarders. Today, it is around fifty. Many of her boarders have been at Diamond D for years, and she always has a waiting list. Jewel's younger sister, Joy Harmon, assists her and lives in the original ranch house near the barns.

Stall rental includes coastal hay, feed, letting out to the fields daily after breakfast, stall cleaning, and use of the tack rooms. The Griffin's daughter, Dr. Tammy Jordan, lives on the property and provides twenty-four-hour vet care for the horses.

Each afternoon, the two pasture gates are opened around 3 p.m. and the horses come in by themselves and go to their stalls to eat. The next morning, they are released from their stalls to race back out to the pastures.

# "THIS IS NOT JUST LAND. THIS IS THE GRIFFINS."

In the course of writing this book, I spent three months interviewing family members and surviving old friends about Sonny Boy and Jewel Griffin and their Diamond D Ranch.

One question I asked was what I should make sure I included so future generations of Griffins would know about their family's legacy.

The following is a sample of their answers.

### Galynna Kittrell Griffin
"I want others to appreciate all the sacrifices it has taken, the long hours of hard labor that have gone into building this ranch, along with the lessons we've learned. It was a team-effort that starred when two people fell in love and never gave up. I hope I can be part of passing this legacy on. This life is not for everyone, but we love what we do. It's been a lifelong commitment."

### Marty Higdon
"There were so many young people at Diamond D who came there and learned life lessons from Sonny Boy, including my dad and me.

You learned how to be a man, learned how to work, learned how to care for his family, and learned what a good wife was to be like the virtuous woman like my Gran Jewel is.

"If you needed something in life and you found your way to the Diamond D, you was going to get what you needed to find. They wasn't going to give it to you, but they were going to help you get what you needed to find."

**Terry Freeman**

"They went through a lot, but they were committed to one another, and they were committed to keeping their family together. Like any family, they had trouble with their kids, but they never let it dim the spirit they held in their hearts to keep everyone together. Their commitment to their family runs to the bone.

"This is not just land. This is the Griffins. When they started out in 1953, I don't think they could ever have imagined this toward the end of their lives. As I look at what they did, the hard work, the effort, and the sacrifice paid off. They can look back with a smile on their faces, good in their hearts, and say this is here because I'm here."

**Jeanne (Neni) Jenkins**

"She is a giving, caring person. The only other person in the whole world I would give this high of credit to would be my mother. Jewel, her nature on the importance of giving and helping other people came from my mother. When you think my mother had thirteen children and she raised them all, you know what a strong person has to be. That's where I'd put Sissy on that pedestal.

"She's an extremely hard worker. Nothing stopped her. She didn't call for her husband to come, or her brother to come. She just took on anything and everything herself."

### Dr. Tammy Jordan

"They had an unwavering love for each other, for the land, and for their family. They put in the hard work in everything they did for many, many years. That's the reason Diamond D is here."

### Tony Higdon

"I just wish everybody could have what I had when I was a child. Not material things. Just that way of life. Just that way of thinking. That way of upbringing. We had freedoms and could do whatever we wanted to as long as the chores was done.

"Granny Jewel was by far the hardest working individual I ever knew in my life. She's the one that created all of that. Big Daddy liked people. If he pulled up to somebody's house, if they needed something, Big Daddy got it for them, whether it was food or what. Big Daddy helped people out."

### Amy Griffin

"They worked their tails off their whole, entire lives to get things where they are. There was never a day that something didn't have to be done. They loved their family. They'd do anything and everything. Despite when one veers off, they still love them. Family is family and you stick together."

### Judge Lance Day

"They went through good times and hard times. But they always kept their family together. I'm sure the Griffin kids had times when Jewel and Sonny Boy would get upset. But they never cut their kids off. It wasn't an option. They were there for them all the way through. It doesn't mean they covered for them.

"I think for future generations of the Griffins, they need to remember that family is family. You have to remember your stock, and the Griffins come from good stock. The Griffins have a great lineage. Their children in the future need to remember that. They're carrying a good name and the best thing they can do for their name is to keep it clean, just like the Griffins have passed it on to them."

## Donnie Wynn

"They've got big hearts and they'll do anything in the world for you. They're just good people. Anybody who came to them and need help, they usually got it."

## Bo Padgett

"They loved each other unconditionally because he couldn't have got away with some of the stuff he was doing if she didn't love him unconditionally. He always wanted his young'uns and grand young'uns to make something of themselves, not just exist."

## Dwayne Addy

"Sonny Boy was just a down to earth man. He was honest. What he told you, he meant it. It was in stone. If he told you he was going to knock the hell out of you, he meant exactly what he was going to do. He didn't back up. If you did things wrong, he would tell you."

## Casey Garner

"They were great role models and examples of people coming from nothing and making a great life, not just for them, but for generations to come. I would hope my grandchildren will know what hard work, perseverance, and a good work ethic will get you. You can have two cents and make it a gold mine as long you work hard, put your family first, and put God in your life."

## Jane Wiggins

"You have to understand these kinds of people that chose this life. They're all about the way it used to be. They are family oriented and care about each other. They take care of each other. They never put out any bull."

"Jewel, she's the most tolerant person on earth. She is the strongest person, mentally, physically, I ever knew. She's tough. She'd outwork two men. You can't be lazy and hang around her."

## Patricia Griffin Wright

"They went out there in the woods to an old log cabin that was two bedrooms and a living room. It didn't even have a kitchen or a bathroom. We had an outhouse until I was six years old. They made a life out of it. Cathy and I always shared a bedroom and then Cathy, Tammy and I shared a bedroom. We didn't have any privacy in that little house. I like to watch "Little House on the Prairie" on television. That's what it was like."

## Pamela Dwyer

"As an avid reader, Ms. Jewel diligently read The Florida Times-Union, books about interesting people, books about horses, and most of all, the Bible and her Catholic devotions. No matter how exhausted she was, or how long a day it had been, she was determined to get her Bible and prayer time in."

## Jodi Griffin Coxwell

"All of the women in our family have been rocks. That means that they tended to things that needed to be tended to. Granny took care of people. When things got tough, she didn't look at the bad, she looked at the good. As for being a rock, she believed in doing things the right way. She believed when family members need you, you quit what you're doing and take care of the family. You quit doing fun things. If you're riding, you quit riding. You feed the horse, but you take care of your family member. You do what's got to be done. Even if it takes you to 10 or 11 o'clock and you have to get up at 6 the next morning, you get up at 6 o'clock in the morning."

**Charles Spencer**

"The biggest thing about Sonny Boy and Jewel is they worked hard. Anybody that took care of 100 horses worked hard. And he had a mess of cattle to take care of, too. They deserve everything they got."

**Alberta Hipps**

"(As a political candidate) there's no substitute for having Jewel and Sonny Boy, and Michael and Galynna on your side because of the sphere of influence. People know they are a family of integrity, and so well thought of as hard working. If you had their blessing, is a real blessing in a lot of ways. You never felt they got involved because they thought you would do something for them. They just wanted good government. And they wanted God-fearing people."

**K'Leigh Griffin Combs**

"I learned from my granny to be a good friend. My granny has been the glue of our family. She's kind of held it together. There's been times that are tough. You work hard for what you get, you don't expect a handout. And you've got to keep something for a rainy day, especially on a farm, because you never know what's going to happen. And you should always keep your faith during the good times and bad."

**Rodney Butler**

"They loved horses. They loved the ranch. And they loved to see people happy. If you weren't happy, you weren't in the right place. There's always been harmony in this place. As many people as she's got down here, it's harmony. There's never been any hard feelings or any conflicts because Mrs. Jewel will deal with that real quick."

**Margaret Durrett**

"I think Jewel was the driving force behind all of this. I just feel that she's the one who made it. She's a very strong woman, but it's tempered with a little bit of manipulation—like most women do—to make

Sonny Boy think it was his idea. I think Jewel had to make him think some things were his idea to get things done.

"I think this was the place I was meant to bring my horse to. I think we're all destined to do things and I think this is where I was supposed to be. Jewel is like a second mother to me, even though we don't have that much age difference between us."

# Yummy. Yummy. Jewel's Favorite Recipes

Jewel Griffin is legendary for always having great smelling food on the stove and putting delicious meals on the table. Over the past seven decades, she has cooked for family, friends, and even strangers who come to her front door.

Here are four of her favorite recipes.

## TURKEY DRESSING

*Ingredients:*

3 turkey wings
1 pan corn bread
1 box Jiffy cornbread mix
4 eggs boiled
1 stick of butter
1 carton chicken broth
3 stalks of celery chopped (medium)
Large onion chopped

*Directions:*

Cook turkey wings until meat falls off bone. Remove bone and chop meat.
Add chicken broth and bring to a boil.
Add stick of butter, let it simmer.
Mix cornbread & jiffy mix together.
Add chopped turkey, onion, celery, and boiled eggs.
Add juice from the turkey.
Heat oven to 350 degrees.
Bake in large pan for 1 hour.

## Ox Tail Soup

*Ingredients:*

2 ox tails
1 can petit cut tomatoes
1 carton beef broth
4 stalks of celery sliced medium
4 carrots sliced medium
2 potatoes cut small
1 large onion chopped
½ bag frozen fork hook lima beans
Salt & pepper to taste

*Directions:*

Cut excess fat off each ox tail.
Cook ox tails until meat falls off bone.
Remove bone.
Add vegetables.
Cook until vegetables are tender.

## Fruit Cake Cookies:

*Ingredients:*

8 eggs
3 cups flour
2 tablespoons salt
1 pound caramelized cherries
1 pound candied pineapple
2 pounds chopped dates
8 cups shelled pecans
2 cups sugar
2 teaspoons baking powder
2 tablespoons vanilla
Cut fruit and nuts

*Directions:*

Mix together flour, salt & baking powder.
Mix in fruits & nuts.
Beat eggs, add sugar.
Work the mixture together.
Scoop out by spoonful onto greased cookie sheet.
Heat oven to 300 degrees and bake twenty to twenty-five minutes.

## FUDGE

*Ingredients:*

2/3 cup cocoa
½ cup milk
1 stick butter
3 cups sugar
½ teaspoon salt
¼ cup margarine
1 teaspoon vanilla

*Directions:*

Mix cocoa, sugar, salt.
Add milk and slowly bring to a bubbly boil, stirring constantly.
Add margarine, vanilla, nuts.
Heat oven to 250 degrees and bake.

CPSIA information can be obtained
at www.ICGtesting.com
Printed in the USA
BVHW072017300522
638444BV00013B/532